The Shift in *Zakat* Practice in Indonesia
From Piety to an Islamic Socio-Political-Economic System

T0317173

THE SHIFT IN *ZAKAT* PRACTICE IN INDONESIA
FROM PIETY TO AN ISLAMIC
SOCIO-POLITICAL-ECONOMIC SYSTEM

ARSKAL SALIM

ASIAN MUSLIM ACTION NETWORK
SILKWORM BOOKS

This publication is partially funded by The Rockefeller Foundation.

ISBN: 978-974-9511-08-4

Published in 2008 by
Silkworm Books
6 Sukkasem Road, T. Suthep, Chiang Mai 50200, Thailand
info@silkwormbooks.com
http://www.silkwormbooks.com

We acknowledge Bonnie Brereton for her editorial assistance.

Typeset in Warnock Pro 10 pt. by Silk Type
Printed and bound in Thailand by O. S. Printing House, Bangkok

5   4   3   2   1

FOREWORD

Problematizing views from within "Islam(s)" in Southeast Asia

In 1953 the late Gustav von Grunebaum organized a conference of leading European scholars of Islam, the first to undertake a historical and critical self-understanding of "Islamic studies." The conference examined relationships among Muslims, and between Islam and various cultures. It found that the assumptions and methods used in fields of study like Islamic history lagged a century behind those used in European history. One year later Bernard Lewis remarked that the history of the Arabs had been written primarily in Europe by historians with no knowledge of Arabic and Arabists with no knowledge of history.[1]

Half a century later, research on the subject has changed. There is an increasing number of studies on Islam written by Muslims who know the faith, the cultures, and the practices in different contexts—the works by Akbar Ahmad, Mahmoud Mumdani, Chandra Muzaffar, and Nurcholish Madjid are just a few examples among many. Also changed is the global context itself. Now perhaps more than ever, "Islam" is more than just a description of a fifteen-century-old faith shared by one-and-a-half billion people. The word has strong emotive qualities for those both within and outside the faith. Two decades ago the late Edward Said wrote, "For the right, Islam represents barbarism; for the left, medieval theocracy; for the center, a kind of distasteful exoticism. In all camps, however, there is agreement that even though little enough is known about the Islamic world there is not much to be approved of there."[2] It is therefore important to understand, from their own perspectives, the contemporary problems that Muslims are facing.

Works in this series, Islam in Southeast Asia: Views from Within, join many other writings on Islam by authors at the periphery of scholarship, using assumptions and methods that may no longer differ from those used in the centers of learning. But if such is the case, how is this series different from the other writings on Islam that are presently flooding the popular and academic landscapes?

To state the obvious, this series addresses Islam in Southeast Asia. In relation to the Islamic world, where the sacred geography, history, and language of the Middle East seems to have established that region as the center, Southeast Asia is clearly seen as the periphery. But it is misleading to conceptualize Southeast Asia as a single sociocultural entity. As is true elsewhere in the world, societies in Southeast Asia are heterogeneous. Muslims in Indonesia and Malaysia, for example, lead lives that differ from those in Thailand and the Philippines because of the different realities facing majority and minority populations in the respective countries. Furthermore, whether Muslims constitute a minority or a majority, their lives differ again when seen in contexts influenced by Javanese culture, British colonialism, Filipino Catholicism, or Theravada Buddhism, among other things. In short, the cultural topography of Southeast Asia is a rich multiplicity.

Consequently, Islam as believed in and practiced by people in the diverse worlds of Southeast Asia is not necessarily singular, since there could be as many Islams as the various contexts that constitute them.[3] The problems facing Muslims in Southeast Asia will therefore vary. Those portrayed by researchers in this series are unusual, and their analysis is at times groundbreaking, but what they underscore is that Southeast Asian Muslims struggle with multiple identities in sociocultural contexts destabilized by globalizing forces. In addition, the fact that this research is carried out by young Muslim scholars is important; the "new generation" factor could explain both the distinctive set of problems these researchers are interested in and the fresh approaches they use.

The "views from within" approach, however, is not without its own potential problems. To engage in studies claiming to be "views from within" is in some ways to guard against the study of "others" as the study of one's own self, because in such a situation writers face other types of realities that are possibly distorted in some other ways. It is therefore important for readers to appreciate the effort researchers make to situate themselves at a distance that gives them a better perspective on the social realities of their subject while retaining their sensitivity towards, and ability to relate to, the people they are studying.[4]

At a time when Islamophobia is on the rise,[5] it is essential to find fresh perspectives that will allow us to understand the new problems and tensions facing Muslims in contemporary Southeast Asian societies, and to articulate the ways in which they negotiate their lives as members of communities of faith in a fast-changing world. This series of studies by young Muslim scholars of Southeast Asia is an important step in this direction.

Chaiwat Satha-Anand
Faculty of Political Science
Thammasat University, Bangkok

Notes

1. Azim Nanji, ed., *Mapping Islamic Studies: Genealogy, Continuity and Change* (Berlin and New York: Mouton de Gruyter, 1997), xii.

2. Edward Said, *Covering Islam* (New York: Pantheon, 1981), xv.

3. Aziz Al-Azmeh, *Islams and Modernities* (London and New York: Verso, 1996).

4. I have discussed the problem of alterity in conducting research on Muslim studies in Chaiwat Satha-Anand, *The Life to this World: Negotiated Muslim Lives in Thai Society* (Singapore and New York: Marshall Cavendish, 2005), 25–26.

5. Akbar S. Ahmad, *Islam under Siege: Living Dangerously in a Post-Honor World* (Cambridge: Polity Press, 2004), 36–39.

CONTENTS

INTRODUCTION

Since the coming of Islam to the area that is now Indonesia some six centuries ago, *zakat* has been practiced as a financial form of worship.[1] By giving a fixed portion of one's wealth to certain recipients in society, one's soul and remaining wealth are purified. Indonesia's New Order regime (1966–1998) under President Suharto witnessed an increased effort to improve the way *zakat* payment is carried out, with some arguing for incorporating *zakat* into the state structure.[2]

Events in the aftermath of Suharto's downfall intensified this shift in *zakat* practice. These events include the issuance of Law No. 38/1999 on *zakat* management that was passed during President Habibie's administration (May 1998–October 1999), the establishment of Badan Amil Zakat Nasional (BAZNAS, the national board of *zakat* agencies) by President Abdurrahman Wahid in 2000, and further technical regulations concerning *zakat* payment. Such events are clear evidence that the political and economic institutionalization of *zakat* in Indonesia is on the rise. Moreover, current demands that only government-sponsored *zakat* agencies be allowed to collect *zakat* rather than leaving it to the conscience of Muslim individuals will only reinforce this.[3]

How did this shift come into being? What are the events, ideas, and actions that may have given rise to it? Is there any particular institution that is primarily responsible for driving this shift? One might argue that since this shift began under the New Order era, Suharto's government should be credited for it.[4] In my view, it is overly speculative to assume that the New Order's approach towards *zakat* administration was the primary impetus for the shift. While the New Order government might have helped engender it, one needs to consider the external factors that led to and intensified this shift, namely the *zakat* agencies that voluntarily organized themselves under one association or *amil*, called Forum Zakat or FOZ.

FOZ was founded in 1997 by 11 *zakat* agencies.[5] Two years later, the number of member agencies had increased to 150.[6] Although formally established more than a decade ago, FOZ has its origins in various company- and Muslim organization-sponsored *zakat* agencies (Lembaga Amil Zakat, LAZ) as well as provincial government organizations of *zakat* agencies (Badan Amil Zakat, BAZ), which were created during the New Order period. Additionally, despite the fact that most FOZ members are government-sponsored institutions (BAZ), LAZ figures played a major role in directing and shaping the programs of FOZ.

Significance of the Study

Little is known regarding the major impetus behind the shift in *zakat* practice in Indonesia. Most studies have overlooked this issue. Many of them pay particular attention to the possibility of *zakat* playing a major role in strengthening the financial sector of Muslim communities.[7] Others focus on the methods of *zakat* collection and distribution used by certain local *zakat* agencies.[8]

While few works argue for the legitimacy of the Indonesian government to officially manage *zakat* collection,[9] there is one study that seeks to offer a solution to the problem of the double burden of *zakat* and tax for Muslims living in a modern nation-state.[10] Although some studies approach the issue of *zakat* management from a political perspective,[11] adequate attention has not been paid to the actual shift in *zakat* practice in Indonesia.

Eri Sudewo's article is perhaps the only one that even mentions this shift.[12] However, his work focuses more on the shift in the diversification of *zakat* agencies than the shift in *zakat* practice in general. Eri bases his argument on the fact that immediately following the inception of *zakat* agencies in the late 1960s, it was government-sponsored *zakat* institutions (BAZ) that solely controlled the administration of *zakat*. Since the

1990s, a great number of *muzakki* (*zakat* payers) submit their payment to private company-sponsored *zakat* agencies (LAZ). Moreover, Eri's work ignores the relationship between the shift of *zakat* practice and the process of Islamization.

This study examines the socio-historical and political situations that have surrounded the shift in *zakat* practice in Indonesia. Viewed in light of the process of Islamization,[13] this shift indicates that the process is continuing. The study not only explores the major motivation behind the shift, it also provides a comprehensive and incisive account of the shift itself. By understanding the shift in the practice of *zakat*, one will be able to comprehend one of the ways that Islamization is taking place and becoming more deeply entrenched in Indonesia. This understanding will contribute to wiser assessments of the ongoing process of Islamization in Indonesia, for this process has not always run smoothly. Indeed, no one can ascertain precisely when this process will be completed. Instead, one may find that there is legal-political dissonance with respect to the institutionalization of *zakat* in Indonesia. For this reason, as will be demonstrated, what has actually happened with respect to this shift is not so much the Islamizing of Indonesia, but rather the Indonesianizing of Islam.

Theoretical Framework

The theoretical framework that underpins this study is the process of Islamization in Indonesia. The term "Islamization" has had a variety of meanings over the course of Indonesian history. Ricklefs's analysis, which views Islamization as a three-phase process, is quite relevant here.[14] According to Ricklefs, during the first phase that spanned the fourteenth to the eighteenth century, the term "Islamization" initially referred to the process of the coming of Islam to Indonesia[15] or the conversion of the indigenous people to the religion of Islam.[16] The term does not simply denote the process of replacing old beliefs with new ones; it also includes

3

the absorption or assimilation of Islam into the local culture, symbols, literature, political institutions, legal texts, traditions, and customs.[17] All these permeations of Islam into Indonesian life were peaceful and almost silent in manner. As a result of this peaceful permeation, a predominantly acculturated Islam appeared and became established, particularly because of the support of political power,[18] rather than the "orthodox" or "scriptural" version of Islam. This acculturated Islam, accordingly, led to what some call a flawed application of genuine Islamic practices, particularly in Java and in West Sumatra, since it mixed certain local customs with Islamic practices.[19]

With this acculturated Islam a new connotation of "Islamization" later emerged. The term came to mean the purification of acculturated Islam, which was considered to be in disagreement with original Islam because it was deeply influenced by local customs. The emergence of this new meaning was possible, thanks, in part, to the return of Indonesian pilgrims from Mecca beginning in the nineteenth century.[20] The pilgrimage to Mecca was quite significant in shaping new features of Islamization since it generated attempts to purify Islamic teachings from *bid'ah* (religious heresies) in order to demonstrate an original commitment to untainted Islam and to fight against acculturated Islam.[21] This new meaning represented the second phase of Islamization in Indonesia, which was marked by tensions and clashes among Muslims themselves.[22]

Purification in the context of the new meaning of Islamization continued until the twentieth century. In fact, as the impact of religious reforms in the Middle East in the late nineteenth century was felt, a number of Islamic reformist movements that held firmly to a more genuine commitment to Islam were established in Indonesia by the early part of the third phase of Islamization.[23] The foundation of the Muslim modernist movements such as Muhammadiyah, Al-Irsyad, and Persis was intended to purify and rectify what was perceived to be a degeneration of religious belief and Islamic practice, including Javanese mystical practices and doctrines.[24]

In light of this purification, Islamization was intended to educate Muslims who nominally already subscribed to the Islamic worldview, so that they would become "true Muslims" (*Muslim sejati*). Education and information were considered the most effective means of advancing this type of Islamization.[25] It is worth mentioning here, however, that the traditionalist Muslim group, Nahdlatul Ulama (NU), which was founded in 1926, did not fully support Islamization through purification. Instead, this group maintained that an admixture of local traditions with the religion did not necessarily contradict the teachings of Islam.[26] Islamization, in the sense of purification, was not NU's main concern. Indeed, it did not see any urgency to launch a program since it saw such local traditions as basically Islamic.

In addition to purification, the meaning of the term Islamization during the late nineteenth century and throughout the twentieth century implied several concepts at different times. Given that a more thorough Islamization of Indonesia was undertaken in a purposeful and organized way only in the twentieth century, a new grouping of periods within the third phase of Ricklefs's classification may be needed. It might be said that there were three periods of Islamization during the twentieth century that continue up until today.

First, there is the Islamization of political institutions, which dates from the founding of the nationalist party Sarekat Islam (SI) in 1911 to the political consolidation of the New Order regime in 1968. This kind of Islamization, according to Muzaffar, became widespread especially in the post-colonial era.[27] Muzaffar further argues that this Islamization is "a part of the reassertion of an identity, which was suppressed under Western colonial rule." Viewed through this lens, "Islamization is an endeavour to establish the uniqueness of a civilisation which refuses to accept Western domination and control."[28] Thus, it is no wonder that some key "Western" political concepts such as nationalism, the nation-state, presidential government, parliamentary democracy, constitutionalism, and the idea of a state political ideology have been the objects of Islamization efforts during this period. Political parties, parliamentary debates, armed struggle, and the 1955 elections in Indonesia were devices to Islamize the country at the political level.[29] These efforts, however, did not succeed for a variety of reasons, as will be later discussed.

Second, there is the Islamization of social life, which focuses on society rather than the state. As described by Salleh, a professor at Universiti Sains Malaysia, the Islamization of society usually refers to the process whereby Islamic culture and values become embedded in society, though it tends to refer more to the ceremonial and ritual level of the individual Muslim, such as observing the main tenets of Islamic teaching in everyday life.[30] In fact, the Islamization of society has not only established a stronger sense of identity among Muslims,[31] it has also improved the level of their distinct economic activity.[32] That is why the effect of this type of Islamization has always been to produce an awareness of self-identity that results in becoming a more observantly practicing Muslim. Although this sort of Islamization has sought to strengthen the religious life of individuals, it does not necessarily imply an increased religiosity of Muslims, let alone an increased role of Islam in Indonesian public life.

The Islamization of Indonesian society took place from 1968 to the fall of the New Order regime in 1998. It emerged when it was clear that all hopes for the Islamization of political institutions were gone. The Islamization of Indonesian society gained momentum after the New Order government suspended all discussions regarding the Jakarta Charter at the end of 1960s, forced all Islamic political parties to be fused into a single party (Partai Persatuan Pembangunan, PPP) in 1973, and by the early 1980s imposed Pancasila to replace Islam as the sole ideological basis of all political parties. As there was limited accommodation of certain Islamic institutions within the state administration during the 1990s,[33] many observed that such depoliticization of Islam by the Suharto regime was a blessing in disguise for the Islamization of Indonesian society.[34]

Realizing that all struggles related to the Islamization of political institutions—particularly the movement towards proclaiming an official Islamic state—had failed, many Islamic leaders began to work from another angle by infusing society with Islamic precepts and thus working toward Islamization from below. Intensive *dakwah* (Islamic preachings) and the publication of great numbers of Islamic books during this period were seen as ways to accelerate the Islamization process.[35] After all, perhaps as an unintended consequence of the New Order's policy of depoliticizing Islam, the state apparatus through the Ministry of Religious Affairs (MORA) had transformed itself into an official agent of Islamization by initiating the incorporation of some aspects of *shariah* into the national legal system.[36] Several Islamic radical groups have regarded this governmental campaign as pseudo-Islamization since it merely accommodated certain Islamic elements in a partial or fragmentary manner. At the same time, the government apparatus itself and certain members of society continued to be dominated by un-Islamic attributes, such as corruption, bribery, fraud, and blackmail.

The re-Islamization of state and society may be seen as the third period of twentieth-century Islamization. In the aftermath of the Suharto regime's fall in 1998, a number of Islamic groups have insisted on Islamizing both the outer form and the inner substance of political institutions, social relations, and the Muslim individual. Because these groups believe that God will observe and evaluate their works as worship, their efforts include establishing Islamic political parties, giving *shariah* constitutional status, promulgating Islamic by-laws in certain local regions, demanding Islamic morality in public life, pushing for full respect for Islamic holidays and events, showing Islamic solidarity towards other Muslim countries, and identifying themselves as truly committed Muslims who practice Islam in all aspects of human social relations.[37] It is most likely that the current efforts of re-Islamization of state and society in Indonesia will follow or resemble what has been going on in other Muslim countries (i.e., governmental campaigns of Islamization such as in Iran, Pakistan, and Sudan during the last three decades).[38]

Given this theoretical framework, the term "Islamization" is understood in this study as a process of specific measures and campaigns that call for the reinstatement of Islamic doctrines in Muslim legal, political, and social systems.

Islamization is often promoted by Islamic group movements who view it as a proactive force for political change and social development. In the particular context of the shift in *zakat* practice in Indonesia, Islamization refers to:

- any attempt that seeks to change Muslims' perception of *zakat* from an act of religious piety to the foundation of an Islamic socio-political and economic system; this change amounts to urging Muslims to pay their *zakat* to a *zakat* agency, instead of directly to *zakat* recipients;
- any means of encouraging the state to be officially and directly responsible for the collection and distribution of *zakat*; and
- any effort that seeks to transform the practice of *zakat* from a voluntary act to a compulsory one, thus penalizing those who are negligent in paying *zakat*.

Methodology

This study is qualitative in nature, relying extensively on documentary data and interviews. It is presented mainly as a case study that focuses on the shift in *zakat* practice in Indonesia. Nearly all of the data collection was gathered in Jakarta, including fifteen interviews conducted with informants.

The units of analysis consist of: (a) historical events related to *zakat* practice in Indonesia as well as views of important figures involved in the shift in this practice; (b) all government policies created since Indonesia's independence, such as the joint ministerial decree in 1991 and Law No. 38/1999 on *zakat* management; and (c) any statements related to the shift in *zakat* practice made by Indonesian government agencies.

The research is comprised of a theoretical overview and an empirical investigation. The theoretical overview includes a literature review of books, journal articles, and academic theses for the purpose of providing a conceptual framework. Empirical research was conducted through fieldwork consisting mainly of observation, documentary research, and in-depth interviews.

For the most part, observation was carried out indirectly by monitoring printed as well as electronic media, especially newspapers, magazines, and websites covering the shift in *zakat* practice. The documentary research was conducted by analyzing government enacted regulations and internal documents published by *zakat* agencies. In-depth interviews were used for gathering information from important persons, including leaders of FOZ and *zakat* agencies such as Dompet Dhuafa, BAZIS (Badan Amil Zakat, Infak dan Sedekah) DKI Jakarta, BAZNAS, and IMZ (Institut Manajemen Zakat). Informal Muslim leaders (*ulama*) closely involved with the issue of *zakat* in Indonesia were also interviewed. Interviews were conducted in 2003, with updates made during July–October 2004.

Structure of the Study

A brief discussion of the Islamic practice of *zakat* and the incorporation of this practice into a modern legal system is provided in the next section, with comparative reference to the Pakistani experience in legislating *zakat*. The purpose of this discussion is twofold: (1) to explain how the shift in the practice of *zakat* turns out to be a means of Islamization, and (2) to show that the shift in the practice of *zakat* has led to dissonance in the legal-political system of a modern nation-state.

The historical background of *zakat* administration in Indonesia is then presented along with how *zakat* was managed from Dutch colonial times through the New Order era. This is followed by a discussion of the origin and emergence of Forum Zakat (FOZ) as well as FOZ's achievements during three periods (1997–1999, 2000–2003, 2003–present).

The enactment of *zakat* law in Indonesia is then explored in depth, particularly under Indonesia's post-New Order regime. The law's enactment represents a structural shift in *zakat* practice and administration. After examining this institutional shift several questions are addressed regarding how the shift in *zakat* practice was maintained and developed during Indonesia's transition years (1998–2004). The study concludes with an analysis of the development of *zakat* in light of the ongoing process of Islamization in Indonesia.

ZAKAT IN ISLAM: AN OVERVIEW

The Concept of *Zakat*

Zakat technically means to give a fixed proportion of one's wealth to certain recipients in society.[39] While its lexicological meaning is "to purify," it also carries with it the connotation of "to grow or increase." What is meant to be purified is accumulated wealth; thus *zakat* is a kind of tax as well as a pious act (*ibadah*). Every Muslim who owns or keeps certain kinds of assets such as gold, silver, jewelry, cash, livestock, and/or agricultural holdings is supposed to pay *zakat* for each one-year period of ownership. Except for agricultural output levied as a tithe, the required duty amounts to 2.5 percent of the value of these assets per annum.[40]

There are two types of assets liable to *zakat*: apparent wealth (*al-amwal al-zahirah*) and hidden wealth (*al-amwal al-batinah*). While the state may forcibly levy *zakat* on Muslims with apparent wealth, those who own hidden wealth are left to rely on their conscience for making the *zakat* payment. These categories of wealth were supposedly introduced by the caliph 'Umar b. Khattab (d. 644), although there was no consensus on what the terms actually meant.[41] Even in the time of the caliph Uthman b. Affan (d. 656), the definition given to "hidden wealth" contradicted its literal meaning, as it included highly visible assets such as housing and slaves. Meanwhile, certain easily concealed goods such as gold and jewelry were deemed "apparent wealth." It seems that this categorization system was driven by the expediency of the time rather than anchored in strictly religious criteria.[42]

The Practice of *Zakat*

In spite of its high position as one of the Five Pillars of Islam, *zakat* is perhaps the religious duty least complied with by Muslims. At least two reasons account for this. First, many Muslims lack adequate knowledge regarding the procedures of when, where, and how to pay *zakat*, regardless of their awareness of their obligation to make *zakat* payment.[43] This lack of knowledge arises out of the common reality that religious teachers in their preachings rarely supply instructions on *zakat*. Moreover, although the literature on *zakat* is extensive, there is no substantial agreement over the practical meaning of the *zakat* requirement. As Timur Kuran, the King Faisal Professor of Islamic Thought and Culture at the University of Southern California, points out: "There has never existed a single source that offers an authoritative account of how *zakat* should be paid or disbursed. . . . [T]he system has never been applied consistently over either time or space. . . . [Indeed], during Islam's first few centuries the application was never uniform."[44]

The lack of agreement over *zakat* practice among Muslims at various times and places is due to the nature of *zakat* itself. The Qur'an does not elaborate on *zakat* administration and enforcement. In fact, there is no clear directive as to whether to centralize or decentralize, institutionalize or personalize the application of *zakat*. Although the Qur'an mentions eight recipients of *zakat* including a *zakat* agency (*al-'amilin 'alayha*),[45] there is no further instruction on how *zakat* should be collected, or whether Muslims are obliged to pay their *zakat* to this agency, or whether they can voluntarily give their *zakat* directly to the poor and the needy.

Another problem for *zakat* practice stems from the multifaceted function of *zakat* as it has developed since early Islam. Given the purpose of *zakat* mentioned in the Qur'an[46] and as a historical response to the necessities of the Medina city-state and circumstances of the poorer Muhajirun (Muslims who migrated from Mecca to Medina),[47] the practice of *zakat* includes spiritual,[48] political,[49] and economic[50] objectives. In its totality, the *zakat* payment purified one's soul and wealth, and supported the socio-political and socio-economic structures that were necessary in early Islam. These three goals, however, are not easily achieved today. In fact, the application of *zakat* in the modern period has never been the same from one Muslim country to another. Practices range from complete incorporation of *zakat* as a regular tax of the Islamic state (Pakistan, Sudan, Saudi Arabia), to the establishment of intermediary financial institutions that receive voluntary payments of *zakat* (Jordan, Egypt, Bahrain, Kuwait, Indonesia), to the marginalization of *zakat* according to the individual's private conscience (Morocco, Oman).[51]

Zakat and Islamization: The Pakistani Case

In what ways could institutionalizing *zakat* turn out to be a means of Islamization? There has been an attempt in some Muslim countries, including Indonesia, to simplify *zakat* practice by subordinating its spiritual function to its political and economic purposes and by centralizing its administration. A shift from conceiving of *zakat* primarily as an act of piety to emphasizing it as the foundation of the Islamic political and economic system is now underway. Likewise, there is strong demand that Muslim governments alone must assume the responsibility "of collecting *zakat* and not leave its payment and distribution to the conscience of individuals . . . for *zakat* is now seen as an entirely viable alternative to the secular tax."[52] In short, centralizing *zakat* administration in government agencies and integrating it into the modern taxation system to improve state revenue and fund a social security system are stages toward deepening the Islamization agenda in Muslim countries. This study views Islamization as a process that includes shifting from a traditional practice of *zakat* collection to a more innovative one, which requires the reinstatement of Islamic doctrine (i.e., *zakat*) in the political and economic system.

At present, six Muslim countries already enforce *zakat* collection: Saudi Arabia, Libya, Yemen, Malaysia, Pakistan, and Sudan. Three of these have referenced the state's responsibility for *zakat* administration in their respective constitutions: Sudan (Art. 10), Yemen (Art. 21) and Pakistan (Art. 31).[53] Of these countries, the Pakistani case has perhaps attracted the most attention by scholars since the administration of *zakat* there has become an exemplary part of the greater agenda of Islamizing the nation-state.[54] The administration and management of *zakat* in Pakistan suggests how *zakat* collection and disbursement is characterized by a centralized structure that serves as a pillar for the economic and political interests of the Islamic state. The Pakistani government's intervention in *zakat* administration does not, however, necessarily guarantee the success of this mode of Islamization in reaching its goals.

After more than two decades since it was first introduced through the *Zakat* and *Ushr* Ordinance No. 17 of 1980, the centralization of *zakat* management in Pakistan is still far from achieving any socio-economic or political transformation.[55] The real lives and economic conditions of millions of Pakistani citizens were completely unchanged by *zakat*.[56] Instead, a great number of socio-religious and political problems have arisen from state involvement in *zakat* administration.

The incorporation of *zakat* into the Pakistani legal system has fixed the nature of *zakat* from a previously voluntary religious duty to one that is compulsory.[57] In fact, the state has instituted "an official version of Islamic law in the face of differences of opinion among members of different schools and sects as to what Islam requires."[58] In the first days after issuing the *zakat* ordinance to all Pakistani Muslim citizens, the ordinance encountered strong opposition from members of the Pakistani Shia community, who argued that the provision of centralized *zakat* violated the right of Shia to distribute *zakat* as dictated by their religious awareness and based on the instructions of their particular understanding towards *shariah* jurisprudence.[59] In April 1981, the government eventually decided to allow Shia Muslims to file for exemption from paying the compulsory *zakat*.[60] This case suggests that it is unrealistic to expect the state to officially acknowledge the practice of only one version of Islam.

The institutionalization of *zakat* formally levied solely on Muslims has only enhanced the growing sense among the minority of non-Muslim Pakistani citizens that the state discriminates against them. The Pakistani government program of Islamization is seen by non-Muslims as a sign that adherence to Islam is becoming the real basis of political community in the country. As such, non-Muslims can only be considered second-class citizens.[61] In this respect, it is clear that the program of Islamizing the nation-state is likely to result in prioritizing particular religious adherents at the expense of other religious communities.

The integration of *zakat* rules into the Pakistani taxation system has transformed *zakat* payment from previously being a simple and easily fulfilled task into something with all the trappings of modern systems of taxation that are difficult to understand for many Pakistanis, particularly the illiterate.[62] The *zakat* law consists of complex rules that adopt the vocabulary of the tax regulations, which are not familiar to the majority of ordinary Muslims. This change has also depersonalized the payment of *zakat*. The government automatically levies *zakat* from bank accounts of Muslim citizens each year during Ramadan. As a consequence, Pakistani Muslims who had previously paid their *zakat* directly to those whom they considered eligible recipients now feel that money payable under the ordinance is just like any other tax demanded by the government. Moreover, some Pakistanis thought that their *zakat* obligation was not yet fulfilled and hence felt compelled to make another, traditional *zakat* payment.[63] This situation illustrates how the spiritual purpose of *zakat* has been absorbed by the overwhelmingly political and economic objectives of the Islamic state that treats *zakat* as a source of official revenue.

As a consequence of the depersonalization and hence the religious delegitimization of *zakat*, many Pakistani Muslims sought to evade all or part of their *zakat* payment. According to Malik, they did so "by not keeping [their] assets in forms taxable under the *zakat* law or by removing assets from the taxing institutions just before the assessment [was] made on the first day of Ramadan."[64] As Malik further explains, a few days prior to the *zakat* deduction date, many Muslim *zakat* payers transferred their funds to the accounts of those who were not obliged to pay *zakat*, like non-Pakistanis, non-Muslims, and Shia citizens. In doing so, they decreased the amounts in their accounts to below *nisab* (the minimum amount liable to *zakat* payment), thus making their funds exempt from the levy. After the deduction date, these funds were transferred back to their original accounts.[65] This state of affairs demonstrates that the formalization of *zakat* payment by the state has eliminated the sincere character needed in performing religious duties. This, in turn, may have led to the spread of payment evasion among Muslims.

The official implementation of *zakat* by the Pakistani government has created competition between political parties for control over the distribution of *zakat* funds. This competition arises from the fact that the *zakat* system has been established at every administrative level, from that of state down to village and town. The local *zakat* committees have fallen under the control of political parties because the committee has become a source of financial support and, under certain conditions, could function as a mobilizing center for the political party.[66] The political repercussions of this *zakat* administration would inevitably diminish the spiritual position of *zakat* as one of the Five Pillars of Islam.

In light of the problems caused by the centralized administration of *zakat* in Pakistan, it is clear that there is dissonance in such formal incorporation of *zakat* into the legal-political system of a modern nation-state. This Pakistani case demonstrates that the belief that Islamization would enhance Muslim religiosity appears unfounded. It is fair to say that *zakat* administration in Indonesia would likely suffer the same fate as in Pakistan if current efforts towards centralizing *zakat* and making it compulsory are realized. Even if the shift in the *zakat* practice in Indonesia is completed, whether this shift will secure spiritual, political, and economic goals remains uncertain.

ZAKAT IN INDONESIA: A HISTORICAL PERSPECTIVE

Dutch Colonial Policy

Little information is available regarding Dutch colonial policy on *zakat* in Indonesia. Most of the information that does exist is restricted to Java and relies much on C. Snouck Hurgronje's correspondence that contains his advice on the problems of *zakat*.[67] As an official advisor to the Office for Indigenous Affairs (*Het Kantoor voor Inlandsche zaken*), Hurgronje advised the Netherlands East Indies government on *zakat* administration in various parts of Java from 1889 to 1906.

Some scholars have referred to this correspondence when discussing the collection and distribution of *zakat* in the colonial period.[68] Their discussions, however, are very limited and do not clearly illustrate how the Dutch policy on *zakat* was implemented. For example, Hisyam has devoted a considerable number of pages explaining how *zakat* was managed under colonial rule; however, he is primarily concerned with the tasks of religious officials in collecting *zakat* in different districts in Java. Moreover, Hisyam does not pay great attention to the Dutch colonial policy on *zakat* in general. Likewise, it is surprising that, although Aqib Suminto's work deals mainly with colonial policy on Islam,[69] it does not touch the issue of *zakat* at all.

The institutionalization of *zakat* in the early centuries of Islam's coming to Indonesia is unclear. There is no evidence that the institution of *zakat* was formally transformed into an official tax regularly collected by a political entity of Muslim kingdoms. Instead, it appears that *zakat* was voluntarily practiced and that Muslims were not compelled to pay it. Hurgronje explained this situation by noting the fact that the process of Islamization in Indonesia was a peaceful one in which the religion was brought by Arab traders and Sufi travelers. In the absence of conquest, no Arabic kingdoms were founded as a result of this spread of Islam.[70]

The nature of *zakat* practice might have been different if Islamization in Indonesia had taken place by Arab conquest, in which case *zakat* would have become a political payment as a form of recognition for Arab rulers taking control of the territory.[71] Thus, it may also be inferred that *zakat* had never been considered a form of Islamic taxation levied as a political payment. It is much more logical to assume that the *zakat* payment was left to Muslims to donate voluntarily. This would have made the position of those who mastered Islamic knowledge—such as religious officials (*lebe'*, *kaum*, *amil*, and *modin* at the village level, and *penghulu* and *naib* at higher levels) and informal religious leaders (*kiai*, *'ulama*, *ajengan*, etc.)—important in handling numerous daily religious affairs, including the collection of *zakat*.[72] It is not surprising then that when a local Islamic kingdom was established, such jobs were left in the hands of those persons. In fact, they were given more opportunity to become involved at the court and in daily governance.[73]

Local rulers, after becoming Muslim, supervised and intervened in those religious affairs.[74] The intervention was merely to help religious officials collect the *zakat* payment from Muslims. Despite this intervention, it may be plausible to assume that Muslim kingdoms in Java never intended to establish official institutions to collect and distribute *zakat*, let alone to force people to pay *zakat*. Indeed, there is little evidence regarding how often the local Muslim rulers themselves paid *zakat*. The records available to us are too obscure to make any kind of judgement on the practice of *zakat* by the Muslim kings. For example, in one case, "at the time of the first organizing of Mataramese land under Senopati (c. 1590) or more probably under Sultan Agung (c. 1625), of each 25 *cacahs* (units) of land, one was reserved for the religious people as *waqf* (endowment), *perdikan*-land, thus as a sort of *zakat* on behalf of the king [sic]."[75] This vague information is problematic, as land itself is not liable to *zakat*. Why then did the Mataram kings reserve land for *zakat*? What kind of wealth did the Mataram kings seek to purify by giving such land as *zakat*? Based on this, it might be fair to say that the practice of *zakat* under the

Muslim kingdoms in Java was not officially organized in accordance with Islamic legal rules.

Given the lack of an official organization overseeing *zakat* administration by the Muslim political entity, it is probably safe to speculate that most shares of *zakat* fell to those *amil* who were directly involved in collecting *zakat* (usually mosque organizers—*modin, naib,* or *penghulu*) and to village Qur'an teachers. Only a small portion was given to those religiously entitled to a share of *zakat,* such as the poor and the needy. In fact, the collected *zakat* gradually became the regular income of local religious officials.[76] This practice was justified by the fact that, as appointed religious officials, they did not receive any salary from the government. Some *zakat* funds, therefore, were claimed as their portion.[77] The local rulers, such as heads of villages, also enjoyed a share of *zakat* to the extent to which they helped in its collection.[78] Such practices in the distribution of *zakat* funds continued up to Dutch colonial times.

The misuse of *zakat* funds for personal benefit by some native officials such as the regent (*bupati*), district chief (*wedana*), and village head (*kepala desa*) created a bad impression in the eyes of the Netherlands East Indies government. Realizing that such abuse by its own appointed officials might disrupt political stability in the colony, the Netherlands East Indies government in 1866 issued a regulation (*Bijblad* No. 1892) prohibiting those officials from being involved in collecting and distributing *zakat.*[79] However, this regulation was only applicable in Central Java, East Java, and Banten; in Priangan and Cirebon such regulations could not be imposed due to the existing vow of the Dutch government commissioner not to interfere with the *penghulus'* earnings.[80] With the support of native officials at their respective levels of government, the situation in Priangan and Cirebon remained unchanged: the *penghulu, naib,* and *lebe'* continued collecting *zakat* from the people.

As a result of the 1866 regulation, there were two different ways in which *zakat* was collected in Java. In Priangan and Cirebon, the *penghulu* with the support of native local officials was actively involved in the management of *zakat* and, hence, more *zakat* could be collected and more abuses by officials were reported. The opposite practice was evident in Banten, Central Java, and East Java where there was no longer any official *zakat* agency (*amil* or *penghulu amil*) collecting *zakat*. Consequently, *zakat* payment was low, as it was paid only by devout Muslims directly and mostly to non-official agencies, such as religious teachers or village Qur'an teachers.[81] Certainly, this regulation did not completely eliminate all abuses in *zakat* practices that remained evident in various parts of Java at the turn of the nineteenth century. The regulation marginally reduced abuses involving government officials. But this achievement was still limited to Banten, Central Java, and East Java. In these regions, there was considerable leeway for Muslims regarding the religious obligation of *zakat* payment, and thus they did not feel compelled to pay it. Consequently, the *zakat* payments received by officials in these regions were very low and accordingly there was virtually no official abuse.[82] The misuse of *zakat* funds was still evident in these areas, but here the government officials were no longer involved. Local religious officials or, more likely, informal religious leaders who were asked to distribute the *zakat* funds might still claim the largest proportion of *zakat*.

Although the diversion of a large portion of *zakat* to a *zakat* agency was considered a deviation from Islamic teachings, Hurgronje advised the government to regard it as a tolerable abuse. For him, the misuse of *zakat* funds might be acceptable,[83] but not if there were abuses of power where local native officials used political pressure or religious officials coerced people to pay *zakat*.[84] Only in these circumstances would formal abuse in the practice of *zakat* collection be considered to have taken place. Since this kind of abuse could create major problems for many people and threaten political stability, the colonial authorities had to prevent officials from using pressure or threats to force people to pay *zakat*.

It seems clear that the meaning of "abuse" suggested by Hurgronje was much more in the area of bureaucratic ethics rather than in religious criteria.[85] And for this reason, so long as there was no formal abuse by government officials and no intimidation by religious officials to force people to pay *zakat*, it was to remain untouched.

Hurgronje felt that while *zakat* payment is obligatory in religious terms, the government should prevent it from being a mandatory payment. Thus, government officials should not be involved, as their involvement would create political pressure on people who would hence feel obliged to pay *zakat*. However, any Muslim who willingly regarded it as a religious obligation and readily handed it over to *zakat* recipients would not be prevented from doing so.[86] In Hurgronje's view, it would be an error on the part of the government to prohibit voluntary *zakat* by Muslims, as such a prohibition would only result in the emergence of a desire on the part of Muslims to engage in what was forbidden. Since he believed that Muslims would gradually abandon their religion, Hurgronje thought that prohibiting activities that would naturally cease to exist was counterproductive.[87]

If Hurgronje did not propose the prohibition of *zakat*, does this mean that he advised the Dutch colonial government on how to manage it? Apparently he endorsed neither the prohibition nor the management of *zakat*. With respect to government management of *zakat*, Hurgronje was, in fact, against it. An illustration from Purwokerto may elaborate his stance. In 1901, Hurgronje was asked to give advice regarding the proposal to include *zakat* funds in the municipal revenue (*dana kotapraja*), which could be used for broad social benefits such as the improvement of public utilities. The expenditure of *zakat* funds for such purposes had initially been legalized in Purwokerto since 1897, mainly for the purpose of eliminating abuse in the collection of *zakat* by native local officials. Some Dutch officials, including De Wolff van Westerrode, considered the idea brilliant and suggested its extensive application in other areas.[88]

Hurgronje responded that it was beyond the government's responsibility,[89] and added in his next letter that regulations like this contravened Islamic *shariah* as well as Javanese custom.[90] His main objection was that such a proposal would create "a new hidden tax" and, therefore, the local government's involvement in the process would indirectly put more political pressure on people to pay *zakat*. The proposal could thus provoke an accusation that the colonial government had arbitrarily changed Islamic Javanese institutions. Another of Hurgronje's objections was that local officials would apply more pressure to augment the results of *zakat* collection from the people. Moreover, there was no sufficient evidence of the misuse of *zakat* funds to legitimize the local government's intervention in *zakat* management. Furthermore, Muslims traditionally regarded *zakat* as a contribution given to appointed recipients; allowing *zakat* for other expenditures would violate this tradition. And fifth, the proposal contradicted existing Dutch policy, religious law, and local indigenous custom.[91] By offering these reasons, Hurgronje hoped to prevent government officials from being blamed as an apparatus of religion because the enhancement of Muslim religiosity was not part of colonial policy. Moreover, he was also concerned with preventing corruption in the matter of *zakat* funds.

It is no wonder then that Hurgronje advised the Netherlands East Indies government to continue distancing itself from government officials and guaranteeing Muslims autonomy in deciding whether or not to pay *zakat* and to freely decide its allocation. The colonial policy ran parallel with Hurgronje's ideas of neutrality and liberty. It appears, on the surface, that what Hurgronje wanted was merely to create the atmosphere of freedom of action, which implied that the colonial state must act neutrally with regard to religion. This policy certainly was not wrong. Nevertheless, if we look carefully, we find that his ultimate objective was to eradicate corruption concerning religious funds by government officials, whether Dutch or native. With the lack of officials' intervention into *zakat* collection, very few people would want to make generous *zakat* payments; thus the amount of *zakat* funds would decline. Consequently, with *zakat* collection yielding such a small amount, the temptation for officials to exploit or to manipulate *zakat* funds would be lessened. This non-intervention principle that paralleled the existing colonial policy thereby had positive consequences for the colonial government.

Given the absence of government intervention (prohibition or management) and the greater freedom available to Muslims regarding their religious obligation, Hurgronje assumed that Muslims would gradually leave behind their religious practices. His assumption was based on the fact that various religious obligations are burdens for Muslims living in the modern era and, accordingly, in an atmosphere of religious freedom, those religious practices would be abandoned. However, there appears to be a gap in the logic of this view. Wouldn't it have made more sense to presume that by making *zakat* obligatory colonial government involvement in *zakat* practice would create a heavier religious burden for Muslims and, hence, lead them to abandon their religious practices and eventually leave their religion? Why was Hurgronje seemingly oblivious to this particular logic? Two interpretations emerge that may account for this.

First, Hurgronje might have overlooked this, for he was aware that this policy would not lead to the abandonment of religious practices. On the contrary, government intervention in *zakat* management would only increase the level of awareness of *zakat*. The reason is that the nature of government involvement was enforcement, which would leave Muslims with no choice except to pay *zakat*. Likewise, it is not necessarily the case that heavier religious burdens would cause Muslims to abandon their religion. In fact, if Muslims had to choose between compulsory *zakat* payment and voluntary conversion to another religion, they would prefer the former, as apostasy is considered the most serious sin in Islam. In my view, this interpretation is flawed because it might only be applicable to more devout Muslims, while those less devout would undoubtedly find an excuse to change their faith. Indeed, as the *zakat* case in Pakistan has proven, instead of enhanced piety, the spread of apathy is often the result.

The second possibility is that Hurgronje ignored this seeming logic because he realized that involvement in *zakat* could result in growing tensions between Muslims and the colonial government. This was particularly true because the government could be accused of triggering a massive conversion of Muslims to other religions, thus causing the deterioration of the political situation given the widespread outrage of Muslim citizens in the colony. Hurgronje did not want to see Muslims retracting their religious commitment because of a situation set up by the government; nevertheless, he expected that, step-by-step, Muslims would neglect their religious practices. This second interpretation is quite convincing, given the fact that the existing Dutch policy on Islam, as Benda puts it, was "neutrality toward religious life." This policy was "the *sine qua non* for pacification and [political] stability" in the colony.[92] After all, Hurgronje was a prominent Dutch figure who argued "against the unwarranted and optimistic expectations of large-scale conversions [of Muslims] to Christianity," an expectation held by some of his compatriots.[93]

It is interesting to note that Hurgronje's advice to the colonial government concerning *zakat* practice had much to do with his view on *adat* (custom). It is widely known that Hurgronje was supportive of the use of *adat* among local Muslims at the expense of Islamic *shariah*.[94] He generally regarded the practice of *zakat* as much more affected by local tradition than religious teachings. For Hurgronje, the Dutch policy on *zakat* collection should be as follows:

> To acknowledge and to protect religious practices wherever possible provided that practices are considered indigenous, not because they are Islamic, that is to regulate such practices after having been sterilized from any abuse and custom that put heavy burdens on people.[95] . . . [to regulate these practices in order] to protect the individual's autonomy from any pressure in collecting *zakat* and *fitrah,* [in determining] their amount, or in choosing the agency that will allocate those religious funds.[96]

Hurgronje also added that the regulation should require the government to make a comprehensive inspection by assuring that "everyone receive his/her rightful portion [of *zakat*] as the *adat* arranges it, and to avoid that lower *amil*s would be given a lesser portion due to the rapacity of upper *amil*s, and to avert the fraud [that may be committed] by the *zakat* agency."[97]

Given Hurgronje's advice, we may distinguish two types of government involvement in *zakat* practice: acceptable and unnecessary intervention. Acceptable intervention consists of all those minimal governmental efforts to protect individual autonomy to pay or not to pay *zakat*, to keep Muslims free to determine the recipients of their *zakat*, and to prevent the *zakat* funds from being corrupted. This minimal intervention is actually neutral, given that it proposes neither the augmentation nor the elimination of *zakat* practice itself. Unnecessary intervention includes involvement of officials beyond acceptable intervention, such as prohibiting *zakat* practices, obliging people to pay *zakat*, and promoting voluntary *zakat* payment in any arrangement. The latter ranges from establishing an official agency to collect and distribute *zakat* funds, to the management of its benefit for public interests, to the release of an instruction manual to be used by Muslims.

Having said this, we can categorize two forms of unnecessary intervention: hard and soft. Hard intervention takes an all-or-nothing approach; that is, either impose *zakat* payment or eliminate the practice of *zakat*. Soft intervention is likely to persuade Muslims to pay *zakat*. However, one might think that there is no difference between hard and soft intervention given that both are concerned about the same issue; that is, the increase of Muslim piety in observing the *zakat* obligation. Yet, if we look carefully at these two kinds of intervention, we can see that hard intervention (i.e., requiring people to pay *zakat*) could result in spreading recusancy among Muslims. Soft intervention (i.e., encouraging voluntary *zakat* payment), on the other hand, might produce an increasing religious awareness among Muslims regarding their Islamic duties. The former case was evident in Pakistan under President Zia ul Haq, while the latter case could be observed in Indonesia under President Suharto.

Based on these types of government involvement in the practice of *zakat*, it may be fair to say that minimal intervention, as advised by Hurgronje, was an attempt to thwart the growing religious awareness among Indonesian Muslims. There was not much awareness of one's *zakat* obligation during the colonial period because many Muslims did not have adequate knowledge of it. This paralleled the reality that there was no extensive campaign by religious preachers or local Muslim teachers regarding the obligation of *zakat*. In addition, various economic burdens and heavy taxation were put on the Muslim people, thereby reducing generosity.[98] *Zakat*, therefore, according to Hurgronje, was mostly driven by a religious compulsion; that is, failure to comply with this obligation would result in punishment in the hereafter. This motivation, however, was very weak and it was not deeply embedded in the minds of Indonesian Muslims.[99]

The rise of religious awareness was the main concern of colonial policy with regard to Islam and Muslims in the Netherlands East Indies colony. Although the Dutch government allowed Islamic worship and Islamic family matters to be practiced, it sought to impede such practices that would increase Islamic awareness and the political potential of Muslim fanaticism. It did so by putting limitations on certain religious institutions.[100] In the case of *zakat*, the Dutch Islamic policy allowed Muslims to practice it and, in fact, issued regulations concerning it, but not for the purpose of promoting religious awareness among Muslims. Instead, as might be seen in the Purwokerto case above, the Dutch adoption of Hurgronje's idea tended to maintain a low level of Muslim piety regarding their *zakat* obligation. As a consequence of the low awareness of *zakat* obligation, Muslims at that time did not face a significant conflict between the two financial obligations of *zakat* and tax.

The colonial policy on *zakat* in due course generated rivalry between religious officials (*penghulu, lebe,* and *modin*), on the one hand, and informal religious leaders (*kiyai, ajengan,* heads of *tarekat,* and Qur'anic teachers), on the other. The contest was about the legitimacy of their status as an *amil* or *zakat* agency. The former perceived that giving *zakat* to the latter constituted support for government opposition because it would result in strengthening the informal religious leaders' economic status and increase their influence over the people, thus diminishing religious officials' authority. As a result, religious officials often complained that their profession would no longer be honored.[101] In contrast, informal religious leaders repeatedly reminded Muslims that submitting *zakat* payment to the officials did not necessarily mean that their religious obligation was accomplished. It was fulfilled if it was paid to the leaders, they claimed.[102]

This rivalry demonstrates that as early as the nineteenth century, no single institution to administer *zakat* existed in Indonesia. This situation continued until the end of Dutch colonization in 1942. During the Japanese occupation there was an attempt to bring the task of *zakat* collection under one institution. In 1943, the *Majlis Islam A'la Indonesia* (MIAI, the pre-war federation of Islamic political parties and mass organizations revived by the Japanese) took the initiative of establishing an Islamic Treasury (*Baitul Maal*) whose task, among others, was to centrally manage *zakat* collection and its distribution. MIAI sought to establish several branches of the *Baitul Maal* throughout Java. But, not long afterwards, MIAI itself was dissolved (in late 1943); thus attempts to organize *zakat* collection into a single administration ended in failure.[103]

In light of this, it is understandable that current Indonesian law on *zakat* (No. 38/1999) acknowledges two different institutions for *zakat* administration: Badan Amil Zakat (BAZ, government-sponsored *zakat* agencies) and Lembaga Amil Zakat (LAZ, informal/private/company-sponsored *zakat* agencies).[104] It may be fair to say that the view that only one central institution must be responsible for managing *zakat* collection in Indonesia is historically unfounded. The presence of both types of *zakat* agencies in Indonesia currently reproduces a rivalry similar to that of the past, although with slightly different drives. Above all, this represents clear evidence that there has never been a single entity in Indonesia that absolutely claims a religious right to collect *zakat* from Muslim citizens. In fact, Indonesian Muslims have many options available regarding the institutions to which they can voluntarily pay *zakat*.

The Early Period of Independent Indonesia (1945–1965) to the New Order Era (1966–1998)

Newly independent Indonesia adopted the Dutch colonial policy and strategy on *zakat*. The Ministry of Religious Affairs (MORA) was established in January 1946 to take the place of the Dutch colonial "Office for Indigenous Affairs" and to continue the colonial policy on *zakat* practice. One of the tasks of this ministry was to guarantee people the freedom to observe their respective religious duties.[105] With regard to *zakat* practice, MORA issued a circular letter (*Surat Edaran* No. A/VVII/17367, dated December 8, 1951), stating that the ministry would not interfere in *zakat* administration. MORA's responsibility was simply to encourage people to observe their obligation to pay *zakat* and ensure that it was distributed properly in accordance with religious teachings.[106] This statement was the first sign of the Indonesian government's stance on *zakat*. It shows that in the very beginning the government never intended to establish an official institution to centrally manage *zakat* in Indonesia, but rather left *zakat* administration in the hands of Muslim society.

A growing passion to make the Indonesian government responsible for the administration of *zakat* was observable in the early years of the New Order regime. During the years of political transition (1966–1968), there was a reemerging demand for the legalization of the Jakarta Charter as an integral part of the preamble to the 1945 Constitution, which could thus serve as a foundation for legislating *shariah* law for Muslims citizens.[107] Although this demand was rejected three times in sessions of the MPRS (Provisional People's Consultative Assembly) in 1966, 1967, and 1968, the Jakarta Charter was still believed to have great influence over the preamble and Article 29 of the 1945 Constitution. This belief was based on the presidential decree of July 5, 1959, acknowledging the Jakarta Charter as a historical document of Indonesia that inspired and was linked with the 1945 Constitution. The belief became stronger given that the Jakarta Charter was considered a source of law in Article 10 of the memorandum on "The Sources of Law and its Hierarchies" submitted to MPRS by the parliament or DPR-GR (Dewan Perwakilan Rakyat Gotong Royong, Mutual Assistance People's Council).[108]

The belief that the Jakarta Charter remained a valid underpinning of Indonesian religious life has led some Muslim leaders to call for government administration of *zakat*. Some prominent Muslim figures as well as Muslim leaders with key government positions—particularly in MORA—formally proposed *zakat* legislation. In the early New Order era, MORA was basically under the control of the Nahdlatul Ulama (NU) Party and, on some occasions, voiced religio-political attitudes at odds with the ruling regime's political agenda.[109] The NU was the least committed of the Islamic parties that proposed amending the 1945 Constitution to reinsert "the deleted seven words" of the Jakarta Charter. Nevertheless, NU still considered the Jakarta Charter (as effected by the July 5, 1959 presidential decree) as a source of Indonesian national law.[110] For this reason, NU figures, such as those who occupied the position as minister for religious affairs in the early years of Suharto's cabinet, felt that specific laws for Muslims in accordance with *shariah* (e.g., *zakat* and marriage) might be achievable.[111]

It is no wonder then that in July 1967, Saefuddin Zuhri, minister of religious affairs and an NU activist, presented a draft *zakat* law to the DPR-GR. The draft was also sent to the ministries of Finance and Social Affairs for feedback. Although the latter never responded, the minister of finance did reply and suggested that *zakat* management would be better regulated by ministerial regulations than by statute.[112] Perhaps because of this suggestion, the parliament (DPR-GR) chose not to discuss the draft *zakat* law presented by MORA. This suggestion may have also inspired MORA a year later, under Mohammad Dachlan's leadership, to issue a ministerial decree (*Peraturan Menteri Agama*, PMA No. 4/1968, dated July 15, 1968) concerning the foundation of the official *zakat* agency, Badan Amil Zakat (BAZ). The regulation stipulated that a governmental *zakat* committee would operate at all administrative levels (district and subdistrict) across the country.

Before it could be properly implemented, this ministerial regulation was indirectly annulled three months later by President Suharto's speech at the Isra' Mi'raj (Prophet's Ascension) celebration on October 26, 1968. Instead of endorsing the establishment of official *zakat* agencies throughout cities and towns in Indonesia, President Suharto co-opted the institution of *zakat* by offering to take over the entire responsibility for collecting and distributing *zakat* on a personal basis as a private citizen.[113] In his official speech, President Suharto said:

As the first step, I would like here to announce to all Indonesian Muslims that I *as a private citizen* am prepared to take charge of the massive national effort of *zakat* collection. . . . From now on, I am *personally* willing to receive *zakat* payments made in the form of money orders from every single Muslim in the country. God willing, I will regularly publicize to all citizens how much money I receive and I will be responsible for its expenditure. I do really expect that this appeal will be paid full attention and will receive positive feedback from the leaders and all Muslims (italics added).

Five days later, President Suharto issued an instruction (*surat perintah*) assigning three high military officers to make all necessary preparations for a nationwide *zakat* collection drive.[114] He also sent a circular (*surat edaran*) to all public offices and local governments suggesting that they establish organizational apparatuses for *zakat* collection in their respective workplaces.[115]

Initially, the minister of religious affairs appeared not to understand the implications of President Suharto's speech. He assumed that the speech corresponded to the ministerial decree on *zakat*. Consequently, that same week, a ministerial instruction (No. 16/1968) on the detailed implementation of *zakat* regulation was released. MORA only came to realize that Suharto objected to the *zakat* ministerial regulation after receiving a letter from the cabinet secretary (Setkab) on December 16, 1968. In response, the minister for religious affairs issued a ministerial instruction (No. 1/1969) in January 1969, compliant with the cabinet secretary's letter, for the revocation of the ministerial decree concerning the foundation of the official *zakat* agency (Badan Amil Zakat). The regulations under the ministerial decree were suspended because the cabinet secretary regarded the *zakat* collection defined in the decree as the exclusive concern of MORA alone without any need for coordinating with other ministries, which he believed was inappropriate.[116]

Following that ministerial instruction, MORA then circulated a letter (No. 3/1969) supporting President Suharto's scheme on *zakat* collection. This letter announced that all *zakat* collected must be deposited in President Suharto's account at the post offices available throughout Indonesia. Suharto's offer to create "a personally centralized system" was thus nothing less than a roundabout way of announcing impending changes to the mechanism already put in place by MORA. In fact, the maneuver in Suharto's speech changed the nature of *zakat* instruction from official and institutional under the ministerial regulation to something informal and personal, concentrated in an individual person.

The operation of a *zakat* agency under the personal auspices of President Suharto continued only for a few years. In 1974, Suharto concluded his role as a national personal *amil* (a person or institution that manages *zakat* collection). The president's last report on *zakat* was delivered in his *Idul Fitri* (the breaking of the Ramadan fast) speech on November 30, 1970. The report stated that over the past two years the collected *zakat* amounted to only Rp. 39.5 million in domestic currency or US$2,473.[117] This meant that since its inception in 1968 on average no more than Rp. 25 million per year had been collected from *muzakki* (*zakat* payers). In Suharto's eyes, this figure was certainly a small amount compared to the number of Muslims in Indonesia, more than 85 million according to the 1971 census. Suharto justified his resignation from the position of *amil* by this low response to his appeal.

It is not the purpose of this study to scrutinize why so little attention was paid to Suharto's appeal but rather to highlight the rationale behind his resignation. What is important to note is that the low turnout rate put forward by Suharto, though it may have sounded plausible, was perhaps to camouflage his real objective of being a provisional *amil*. One may argue that Suharto's ultimate goal of being *amil* was to fulfill his short-term political interest; that is, to thwart the efforts, in part at least, of MORA to implement the Jakarta Charter by establishing an official *zakat* agency at both the national and local levels of governments. Once his real objective was achieved, there was no need for Suharto to continue collecting *zakat*.

One may wonder whether such a short-term political interest was the real motive behind President Suharto's move based on the fact that after his resignation as the national personal *amil*, Suharto created a foundation in 1982 known as the Yayasan Amal Bakti Muslim Pancasila (YABMP, the Pancasila Muslim Charity Services Foundation) with the specific purpose of developing socio-religious resources for Muslims. This foundation levied almsgiving (*sedekah*), not *zakat*, from all Muslim civil servants in Indonesia by automatically withholding small amounts of their monthly salaries. The foundation spent the collected funds building hundreds of mosques throughout the country.[118] Given that the concept of *sedekah* is very similar to *zakat* in Islam, one may safely argue that President Suharto had established a new *zakat* agency, though in a different way.

One important question is why didn't Suharto, as *amil* in the late 1960s and early 1970s, collect *zakat* in the same way he levied almsgiving through his foundation? If the voluntary *sedekah* could be imposed by the president's foundation, would it not be much easier for him to forcibly levy a compulsory religious duty (i.e., *zakat*) on government employees? It seems very likely that he was motivated by politics.

As Suharto ceased to be a national personal *amil*, there was virtually no appropriate legal basis for the government-sponsored or semi-autonomous *zakat* agencies that he had created. Their only legal basis during that time was Suharto's circular letter issued following his Isra' Mi'raj speech, which suggested founding an organizational apparatus to collect *zakat* in the respective host institutions of *zakat* agencies. When Suharto withdrew from this duty, the question was whether his circular letter would remain valid. The impact of his maneuver was severely felt at that time as it dissolved the legal basis of *zakat* collection in Indonesia, leaving the *zakat* agencies without a foothold. With no judicial foundation or clear national guidance, these *zakat* agencies had to strive to struggle locally.

Surprisingly, although there was no national policy as to the direction in which *zakat* collection would go, the number of *zakat* agencies gradually increased. Abdullah notes that even after Suharto's resignation as *amil*, a great number of provincial administrations established government-sponsored *zakat* agencies, including the following: BAZIS (Badan Amil Zakat, infak dan Sedekah), DKI Jakarta (1968), East Kalimantan (1972), West Sumatra (1973), West Java (1974), South Kalimantan (1974), South Sumatra (1975), Lampung (1975), Irian Jaya (1978), North Sulawesi (1985) and South Sulawesi (1985), among others.[119] In addition, since 1986, a new type of *zakat* organization has emerged: private company-sponsored *zakat* agencies (e.g., the Bontang LNG Company, Pertamina).[120] Another type of *zakat* agency that emerged in the early 1990s was one created by Muslim community organizations (e.g., Dompet Dhuafa Republika, Pos Keadilan Peduli Umat, Yayasan Dana Sosial Al Falah, Muhammadiyah, Persatuan Islam). Yet, the traditional *zakat* collection and distribution mechanism of establishing temporary *zakat* committees by mosque administrators or giving *zakat* directly to the poor is still widely found in Indonesia [121]

Since 1989, the Ministry of Religious Affairs has sought to encourage a variety of *zakat* agencies. From this time onwards, in conjunction with the shift in a national political configuration that favors the Muslim community, the general policy on *zakat* was gradually established even though its ultimate goal was still unclear. MORA realized that the time was not ripe to propose any formal legislation on *zakat*, let alone to set up a government body as an official national or local *amil*.[122] Aware that President Suharto was not enthusiastic about the formal involvement of government officers in *zakat* administration,[123] MORA could do no more than provide broad guidance and offer limited assistance in the form of ministerial instructions (Nos. 16/1989 and 5/1991) and joint ministerial decrees (Nos. 29/1991 and 47/1991) to the existing *zakat* agencies.[124]

Although this guidance provided a legal basis for the existence of *zakat* agencies in Indonesia, it actually weakened the formal attachment of *zakat* agencies to the provincial government structure. From then on, the governor functioned merely as a patron of *zakat* agencies and could no longer directly engage himself in the *zakat* collection. The regulation thereby changed the nature of *zakat* agencies from established, govern-ment-sponsored agencies to non-governmental and semi-autonomous local agencies. The provincial government had the right to validate the *zakat* agency established by Muslims but not to initiate its foundation. Although the existence of non-governmental provincial *zakat* agencies was acknowledged, and some partial regulations for *zakat* collection were arranged, there was no national agency that centrally organized the collection of *zakat* in Indonesia.[125] In the end, *zakat* payment still remains voluntary.

Despite the current situation, the issuance of a number of *zakat* regula-tions during Indonesia's New Order resulted in the increased awareness of many Muslims of their *zakat* obligation. The willingness of President Suharto to personally manage *zakat* collection during the early years of his regime symbolized his piety as a Muslim, thus popularizing the institution of *zakat* among Muslim citizens. While his stance on *zakat* collection was ambiguous at best, he indirectly promoted the practice of *zakat*, if only for a short period. In the early 1990s, he turned down a request from MORA and MUI (Majelis Ulama Indonesia, the Indonesian Council of Islamic Scholars) to be an official *amil*, while at the same time allowing the facilitation of *zakat* management by ministerial decrees. As all of these actions clearly contradict state policy based on Pancasila—that is, neutrality towards religious life—this trend indicates some support for the Islamization agenda.

Although Suharto's policy on Islam, in general, followed Hurgronje's advice,[126] the same was not true of his stance on *zakat*. While Hurgronje attempted to prevent the government apparatus from being involved in encouraging Muslims to pay *zakat*, Suharto engaged himself in the task of *zakat* collection and thus made himself religiously responsible for properly organizing it. Although Suharto's involvement was as a private Muslim citizen, the fact that he was a leading national figure certainly set a standard for many Indonesian Muslim citizens about exemplary Islamic piety. Indeed, the level of Muslim devotion regarding their *zakat* obligation increased overall during the New Order era.

Zakat and Tax: A Double Burden for Muslims

While Muslims' awareness of their religious duty to pay *zakat* increased during the New Order, at the same time this duty overlapped with their obligation to pay tax to the government of Indonesia. Many Indonesian Muslims are greatly concerned over this double fiscal burden. Responding to the problem, the Indonesian Council of Ulama (MUI) held a seminar on *zakat* in 1988 and affirmed that *zakat* and tax are different duties, and that Indonesian Muslims are obliged to pay both. The reason underlying this view is that *zakat* is a religious obligation mandated by God through the Qur'an and Sunnah to all Muslims, while tax is a duty required by the nation-state but religiously justified based on the principle of public interest (*al-maslahat al-'ammah*).[127] This opinion has certainly burdened Muslims with dual responsibilities. As a result, many Muslims overlook the *zakat* payment but pay tax.

MUI's view concerning *zakat* and tax was challenged by Masdar F. Mas'udi, a leading Nahdlatul Ulama intellectual. In his controversial book, *Agama Keadilan: Risalah Zakat (Pajak) dalam Islam,* first published in 1991, he proposes the idea of simply paying tax as a replacement for *zakat*. According to him, a Muslim who has paid tax is no longer obliged to pay *zakat* since the paid tax is intended (*diniatkan*) to be the *zakat* payment.[128] For Mas'udi, "*Zakat* internally is a human spiritual commitment to God, while externally it is in fact a tax; that is, a human social commitment to others. *Zakat* and tax, therefore, are one and the same." To use the metaphor of the human body, "*Zakat* is the soul and tax is the body that together come to life. The soul (*zakat*) and body (tax) are distinguishable but not to be separated; they have to be integrated."[129]

With the spirit of *zakat* instilled in taxes, Mas'udi puts forth three proposals. First, Muslim taxpayers should no longer view their taxes as a secular obligation to the state, but as a requirement of belief in God, because the state upholds (or should uphold) universal justice, especially for the poor and the needy. Second, there will be a shift in the perception among Muslim taxpayers from conceiving of the state as an almighty entity, capable of repressing them, to the view that the state is only the *amil* and must serve the interests of its citizens. Third, there will be a growing awareness among Muslim taxpayers that they have legitimate rights to supervise the government in administering tax funds. In this way they will ensure that tax/*zakat* funds are spent appropriately for the welfare of all the people, especially the most helpless among them.[130] Mas'udi's view is revolutionary compared to the existing practice of *zakat* and tax in Indonesia. Not surprisingly, his vision has been criticized by other Muslim scholars as well as *zakat* agencies.

One major criticism is Mas'udi's idea mandates that religious obligation (*zakat* as a tax) be authorized by the state, requiring the foundation of an Islamic state given that only a religiously qualified government should levy *zakat* as a tax from Muslim citizens. For many Muslims, while the Indonesian nation-state may be called a Muslim state since the majority of its population is Muslim, it certainly does not meet the criteria of an Islamic state. Therefore, these Muslims cannot accept the notion that a non-Islamic state can require its citizens to practice religious teachings such as *zakat*. In their opinion, Mas'udi's thought implies the Islamization of the nation-state.[131]

This interpretation of Mas'udi's thinking is erroneous. By integrating *zakat* and tax, what he intended was not the unification of two equal institutions or bodies that result in the foundation of a formal Islamic state, but merely the integration "between soul and body, morality and action, or vision and institution." Illustrating his point of view, Mas'udi says:

The essence of the moral commandment of *zakat* is as follows: if with taxes the state builds, then build for the sake of Allah in the interest of the welfare of all the people, especially the weakest; if with taxes the state funds a bureaucracy and pays its civil servants, then let there be the bureaucracy and civil servants who for the sake of Allah loyally fulfill the needs of the people, especially the weakest; if with its taxes the state feeds the servants of the law (police, prosecutors, judges, and so on), then let there be servants of the law who honestly for the sake of Allah protect the rights of all the people, especially the weak; and if with its taxes the state feeds its soldiers and arms them, then let there be soldiers who for the sake of Allah loyally guarantee the security of all the people, especially the weak.[132]

This argument actually is intended to overcome the problematic relationship between state and religion. In Mas'udi's view, although religion and the state are indeed different, they cannot be separated: "religion gives direction, the state gives form." While religion speaks of justice and the common good of all as a trust from God, the state speaks of matters of institutions for that trust and of making it a reality.[133]

It is also argued that Mas'udi's thought on *zakat* and tax is not applicable to the Indonesian context due to the problems associated with distribution mechanisms. As the allocations of *zakat* and taxes are different, the use of tax (*zakat*) funds for the benefit of particular religious adherents may generate an objection from people of other religions. On the one hand, many Muslims believe that a portion of *zakat* (tax) cannot be given to non-Muslims, except for *muallaf* (new converted Muslims). On the other hand, the fact that most tax funds stem from non-Muslim taxpayers, whose tax amounts are larger than Muslim taxpayers, will raise concerns if most of the tax is spent on Muslims. As the majority of Indonesians who live in poor economic condition are Muslim, they are the most eligible to receive the benefit of such funds.

For Mas'udi, this problem is not substantive since it is within the area of *ijtihad* (the use of individual reasoning in matters of *fiqh*). In fact, it can be solved by reaching a consensus among citizens themselves based on their particular situations. What is important is that the decision made must reflect the principle of *zakat*, namely justice and the universal good where those who are able can fulfill their obligation to assist the weak and fund matters of public interest.[134]

It is also feared that Mas'udi's proposal would result in the elimination of existing *zakat* agencies, because it is assumed that the Taxation Service Office (Kantor Pelayanan Pajak) under the auspices of the Directorate General of Taxation, which operates in every district throughout Indonesia, would take over the functions of *zakat* agencies. According to Mas'udi, this would not be the case since all the *zakat* agencies are still needed to collect alms (*sedekah*) and donations (*infak*), the total of which may be much more than *zakat*, especially because *zakat* is paid annually while alms and donations can be given at any time. Certainly, those agencies need to withdraw the term *zakat* from their institutional name (e.g., Badan Amil Zakat, Infak dan Sedekah, BAZIS) and let only *sedekah* and *infak* remain.[135]

Given these objections to Mas'udi's view, and the feeling that MUI's opinion regarding *zakat* and tax is a heavy burden, a breakthrough has been constantly sought. It was Dawam Rahardjo, a Muhammadiyah intellectual who, at the national meeting of the government-sponsored *zakat* collection board (BAZIS) in 1992, first put forward the idea that *zakat* payment could be tax deductible.[136] The idea was supported by the regional *zakat* agency of the Jakarta government and of Central Kalimantan, and attracted attention at a national seminar held in Jakarta by the Faculty of Syariah, State Islamic University, on March 25–26, 1997. The seminar suggested that Muslims who paid *zakat* should be able to claim a tax deduction of at least 2.5 percent. For some, this notion is a compromise between MUI's and Mas'udi's thoughts on *zakat* and tax. Even if *zakat* and tax are considered different entities, they are related. Malaysia has been cited for its exemplary management of *zakat* in this way. However, the practice in certain Western countries, like the United States and Australia, where an individual or public company that makes donations to registered charity foundations is entitled to a tax deduction, is surely to have inspired this notion in Indonesia.[137]

The idea of tax deduction is not unknown in the Indonesian context. The 1925 Company Tax Ordinance and 1944 Income Tax Ordinance stated that every donation given to certain social institutions appointed by the minister of finance could be eligible for a tax deduction. Given this regulation, it was no wonder that in 1976 the minister of finance issued a decree to reinvigorate the ordinance. Three years later in 1979, the general directorate of taxation circulated a letter suggesting that *zakat* payment made to a *zakat* agency be seen as a tax deduction.[138] In fact, this idea is clearly stated later in both *Zakat* Law No. 38/1999, Art. 14[139] and Tax Law No. 17/2000, Art. 9,[140] even though its translation into practice has not been as easy as putting it in writing.

THE RISE OF FORUM ZAKAT

The emergence of Forum Zakat (FOZ) and its role in *zakat* administration helped lead and intensify the shift in *zakat* practice in Indonesia. The organization's importance rests on the fact that it brought various *zakat* agencies into united entities and articulated their aspirations, which sometimes went against *zakat* policies issued by the government, particularly the Ministry of Religious Affairs.

The Origin of Forum Zakat

The rise of Forum Zakat (FOZ) can be traced back to a seminar conducted by Dompet Dhuafa Republika (DD) on July 11–12, 1997 at the Sahid Jaya Hotel in Jakarta. The main theme of the seminar was "*Zakat* of the Public Company." More than one hundred representatives of *Baitul Maal* (Islamic Treasuries) from various private companies and state-owned firms attended. Soon after the seminar, there was an agreement to set up as an association called "Forum Zakat." On September 19, 1997, eleven *zakat* agencies,[141] acting as the founding institutions of Forum Zakat, agreed to register FOZ as a foundation (*yayasan*); this was done through a public notary.

Although FOZ now comprises more than 150 members of BAZ (government *zakat* agencies) and LAZ (non-state *zakat* agencies), the position of Dompet Dhuafa Republika is central since it was the leading institution in the early establishment of FOZ. In addition, even though there were eleven institutions that were formally involved in establishing Forum Zakat, certain prominent figures from those institutions who actively initiated and arranged all preparations in founding FOZ should be mentioned: Eri Sudewo,[142] Abdul ad Muin,[143] Hilman,[144] Aminuddin Daim,[145] Hadi Tjahyono,[146] Iskandar Zulkarnaen,[147] Ismail Yusanto,[148] and Agus Sarwanto.[149]

Despite the fact that FOZ was formally designed to be an association of both LAZ and BAZ, LAZ soon dominated most of FOZ's activities. FOZ then became a representative group of LAZ rather than BAZ. In fact, all FOZ chairmen since its foundation in 1997 (i.e., Eri Sudewo, Iskandar Zulkarnaen, and Naharur Surur) have come from a LAZ background.

By and large, the goal of this association, in the absence of a national *zakat* board, was to create an umbrella organization for various local, provincial, and government-sponsored *zakat* agencies of state-owned firms, private companies, and Muslim organizations. As an association of *zakat* agencies at the national level, FOZ plays an important role in networking and mediating *zakat* issues with the government, disseminating information, raising awareness among Muslims, coordinating activities, and consulting on various *zakat* problems. In short, FOZ aimed to have consultative, coordinative, and informative functions, by which it could enhance the quality of both *zakat* administration and *zakat* agencies in Indonesia.

The diagram on page 43 illustrates the role of FOZ in Indonesia's *zakat* administration.[150]

The Role of Forum Zakat

The vital role that FOZ plays is that of an institution with the authority to verify the status of a non-state *zakat* agency prior to an accreditation process conducted by the Ministry of Religious Affairs. A technical regulation (i.e., the ministerial decree on *zakat*) acknowledged FOZ's important position.[151] With this authority, FOZ became the single legitimate institution that issued a certification regarding whether or not a non-state *zakat* agency is qualified to go through the accreditation process. The status of being an accredited *zakat* agency is important, for it means that a non-state *zakat* agency would be permitted to formally issue a *bukti setor zakat* (a receipt of *zakat* payment), which can be used for tax deduction purposes. At least sixteen LAZ have been accredited by MORA.[152]

One may wonder why FOZ has been given this special authority in light of its shortcomings. Although FOZ is an association of *zakat* agencies in Indonesia, its legal basis is not really strong; it is merely a private foundation (*yayasan*) and not a state institution. Unlike the Council of Ulama (MUI), for instance, FOZ is not well known to Indonesian Muslims. The foothold of FOZ is mainly in Jakarta, while it has few branches outside the capital. Moreover, most members of the FOZ management board were recruited from LAZ itself. One may therefore speculate that conflicts of interest might arise in FOZ's issuing the verified status of LAZ.[153]

From the First to the Third Congress

FOZ organized its first congress in Jakarta on January 7–9, 1999. This congress elected Eri Sudewo, whose institution, Dompet Dhuafa Republika (DD), had since 1997 led the FOZ presidium, a collective body comprised of the eleven founding institutions. The congress established several short-term goals including the legal enactment of *zakat* administration; the introduction of FOZ throughout Indonesia; the identification of all *zakat* agencies in Indonesia, including the creation of networks between them; the publication of manuals on *zakat* administration; and the designation of various programs for economic empowerment. The most important of these—to urge the government to enact the governing rules of *zakat* in the form of a statute—was achieved by September 1999.[154]

Although a *zakat* bill was expected to be finalized at this congress, the prominent role of a national *zakat* board (BAZNAS) in the draft bill was not wholeheartedly welcomed. DD opposed including such a provision. In fact, DD was successful in steering the meeting of the congress (Commission A) to formulate a conclusion stating the disadvantages of such a national *zakat* agency. Three reasons were offered to support this conclusion: (1) BAZNAS was considering centralizing the collection of *zakat*, which would only benefit the center at the expense of the periphery, and thus many

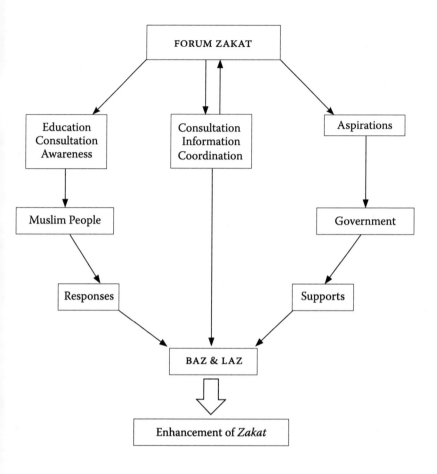

problems in the distribution of *zakat* would emerge; (2) the presence of a national *zakat* agency would be a disincentive to the growth of local *zakat* agencies; and (3) based on Malaysia's experience, there was no need to establish a national *zakat* agency.[155]

Instead of a national *zakat* board, DD preferred to have a federation of *zakat* agencies. FOZ, therefore, was considered an appropriate independent national association of *zakat* agencies since it included those of provincial governments (e.g., BAZIS DKI Jakarta), state-owned firms (e.g., BAZIS

Pertamina), private companies (e.g., Baitul Maal Muamalat), Muslim organizations (e.g., LAZIS Muhammadiyah), Islamic foundations (e.g., Yayasan Dana Sosial Al-Falah), mosques or *pesantrens* (e.g., Masjid Raya Pondok Indah), and non-governmental organizations (e.g., Pos Keadilan Peduli Ummat). The diversity of these *zakat* agencies (seven models) suggests that the administration of *zakat* in Indonesia is not monolithic.

During the early years of FOZ's founding, DD attempted to dictate its defense of the interests of non-state *zakat* agencies (LAZ). For DD, the existence of FOZ was crucial since through this association the non-state *zakat* agencies could have a bargaining position vis-à-vis *zakat* policies officially issued by the Ministry of Religious Affairs. In the eyes of DD, the government-sponsored *zakat* agencies (BAZ), which were established by the provincial governments or by the Regional Office for Religious Affairs, were not creative and, hence, were less productive. The arrogance of this DD assessment reflected the competition between private and government-initiated *zakat* agencies.

Following the enactment of the *zakat* law in September 1999, the Second Congress of FOZ was held in December 1999 in Batam, Riau to follow up on further technical issues arising from the law's enactment. In this congress, FOZ expanded its functions to include both improving the knowledge of those who run the *zakat* agencies and advocating and mediating the interests of its members with other related entities, such as the government.

The Second Congress of FOZ was held only eleven months after the first congress. Eri Sudewo's tenure as chairman of FOZ was very short; he was elected as a chairman at the First Congress of FOZ in Jakarta (January 7–9, 1999) and resigned during the Second Congress at the end of the same year (December 23–25, 1999). The congress elected Iskandar Zulkarnain, director of PT Internusa Hasta Bakti, one of the founding institutions of FOZ, and Ismail Yusanto, a spokesperson of Hizbut Tahrir Indonesia, to be the chairman and vice chairman respectively, for the period 2000–2003. It was not clear why most members of FOZ no longer preferred Eri Sudewo, even though he was one of the candidates selected by the participants at this congress to lead FOZ for at least the next two years.

The stance of FOZ towards the presence of Badan Amil Zakat Nasional (BAZNAS, the national board of *zakat* agencies) changed during the period of Iskandar Zulkarnaen (2000–2003). FOZ previously, under Eri Sudewo's leadership, had been opposed to the emergence of BAZNAS. Now as Iskandar Zulkarnaen assumed the top post as chairman, FOZ reversed its earlier position and began supporting the establishment of BAZNAS. FOZ reportedly helped the foundation of BAZNAS by approaching the state secretary (*Sekretariat Negara*, often abbreviated *Setneg*).[156] The state secretary's approval was necessary for founding any initiative concerning Islamic institutions (especially *zakat*) in Indonesia. In this case, FOZ had successfully convinced the state secretary that BAZNAS was a required institution as stated in the *zakat* law.[157]

In early 2002, FOZ began proposing an amendment to the *zakat* law. FOZ seemed to be aware that *zakat* would not be collected unless the law was amended, specifically by making *zakat* a legal obligation for Muslims and centralizing its administration. On January 28, 2002, FOZ met with parliamentary members to request that the *zakat* law be amended. This request was turned down.

Iskandar Zulkarnaen concluded his tenure as chairman of FOZ at its Third Congress, which was held in Balikpapan on April 25–28, 2003. This congress elected Naharus Surur to assume the leadership of FOZ for the period 2003–2006. Prior to occupying this position, Naharus Surur had headed PKPU (Pos Keadilan Peduli Ummat), a *zakat* agency with a close affinity to the Prosperous Justice Party (Partai Keadilan Sejahtera, PKS).[158] During his tenure, Naharus Surur sought to continue certain agenda items laid down by his predecessor such as amending the existing *zakat* law and empowering BAZNAS. These two issues became important tools by which to deepen the ongoing process of Islamization in Indonesia.

Under Naharus Surur's leadership, FOZ appeared inclined to take part in Indonesia's political affairs. This is understandable since both Naharus

Surur and Ahmad Juwaini (secretary-general of FOZ) are activists in the Prosperous Justice Party.[159] The fact that FOZ was brought into the political arena was apparent prior to the April 5, 2004 election. For FOZ had organized a national dialogue on *zakat* practice on March 4, 2004, inviting political parties to speak on *zakat* with particular reference to the post-election government.[160] Moreover, several weeks before election day, FOZ issued a press release in the Muslim newspaper, *Republika*, suggesting that Muslim voters should not vote for bad politicians (*politisi busuk*).[161] Although this press release sounds innocuous, obviously its implicit message was that of encouraging voters to support the Prosperous Justice Party, which had launched the issue of a "clean and caring" (*bersih dan peduli*) party during the campaign period. As a non-political association of *zakat* agencies, FOZ was not supposed to get involved in any political activities.

The rise of FOZ as an association of *zakat* agencies was significant during the years of Indonesia's political transition. FOZ has been a major player in constructing the structural and institutional shifts in *zakat* practice in Indonesia. Since 1999, the practice of *zakat* has been formally acknowledged in the state structure through the enactment of Law No. 38/1999 on *zakat* management. The law requires a state *zakat* agency to be institutionalized at both the national and local levels. Certain provisions in that law have given many opportunities to pay and develop *zakat* productively.

THE STRUCTURAL SHIFT IN *ZAKAT* PRACTICE

The structural shift in *zakat* practice in Indonesia largely took place in the form of the enactment of the *zakat* law.[162] Although the current *zakat* law seems little more than an extended version of the joint ministerial decree of 1991, the Indonesian government considered this enactment as structural assistance since it repositioned the previous regulation on *zakat* to a higher level (from a ministerial decision to a statute) and upgraded the status of *zakat* agencies from private to government institutions.

The *zakat* law represented a shift in *zakat* practice in Indonesia because it promoted the establishment of official *zakat* agencies (BAZ) from the national level to the district level. There is no hierarchy or subordinate position since BAZ at each level is independent of one another. In addition, each BAZ is allowed to have its own *zakat* collector units (Unit Pengumpul Zakat, UPZ), whose task is to collect *zakat* payment from *muzakki* (*zakat* payers) who reside within their particular area.[163] The law also delineated a number of roles that the government (i.e., the Ministry of Religious Affairs) might play. In this case, the government could take part in *zakat* administration as an institution that issues policies (regulator), raises Muslims' awareness (motivator), provides *zakat* manuals (facilitator), and organizes activities among inter-*zakat* agencies (coordinator). Finally, the law formally stated the relationship between *zakat* and tax by providing a tax deduction for *zakat* payments. For some, this might appear peculiar in a non-Islamic state such as Indonesia.

The Enactment of the *Zakat* Law

The legal drafting of the Indonesian *zakat* law, which began more than thirty-five years ago, has not been easy. The existing law is actually the sixth draft prepared by the Ministry of Religious Affairs.[164] Its first draft was presented to DPR-GR in 1967, but it was withdrawn before parliament had the opportunity to discuss it. Another draft, composed by a joint committee of the Ministry of Justice and the Ministry of Religion, appeared in 1985. However, no follow up was made to transform the draft into a bill that would be presented to DPR. What MORA produced in 1991 was only a joint ministerial decree, which had limited influence on the institutionalization of *zakat* at the regional/provincial level.

At a national meeting of all provincial *zakat* agencies facilitated by MORA in Jakarta on March 3–4, 1992, many delegates from various parts of Indonesia expressed their concern over the necessity of a higher *zakat* institution to organize or facilitate *zakat* nationally.[165] They also requested that Rudini, the former minister of internal affairs, be the chairman of the national *zakat* board. Rudini agreed, but only so long as the existing regulation allowed him.[166] The proposal, however, ultimately ended in failure because of President Suharto's opposition.[167]

It was only after Suharto's downfall in 1998 that the effort to enact a *zakat* law in Indonesia began to gain momentum. Despite the fact that in 1998 MPR's (People's Consultative Assembly) Decree No. X/MPR/1998 on religion and socio-cultural aspects implied that only *hajj* (pilgrimage to Mecca) services would be enacted, MORA thought that there was an opportunity to legislate *zakat* as well. Therefore, soon after President Habibie signed the Bill of Hajj Services on May 3, 1999, MORA finalized the legal draft on *zakat* and obtained a letter of *izin prakarsa* (permission to initiate legislation) from the state secretary on May 15, 1999.[168] Based on this letter, the bill was presented to DPR on June 24, 1999 and began to be discussed on July 26, 1999 at the Bamus meeting of DPR.[169]

The current enactment of *zakat* law resulted from the contributions of both MORA and FOZ, even though the former actually sought to dominate the enactment process. MORA was solely responsible for drafting the bill and conveying it to parliament for approval. It was wary of any criticisms by Muslims or others of the bill. For example, MORA tried to prevent the participation of certain prominent figures from contributing their views, such as Masdar F. Mas'udi[170] and Eri Sudewo who had been outspoken concerning *zakat*.[171] In a seminar on the dissemination of the bill at the Treva Hotel in Jakarta, on August 18, 1999, Masdar said that Malik Fadjar, the minister of religious affairs for the Habibie government, had asked him personally to refrain from criticizing the bill,[172] effectively muzzling his public criticisms.

Likewise, as chairman of FOZ, Eri Sudewo was confused by MORA's invitation to have him discuss the bill on May 14, 1999, without a copy of the proposed law attached. When he finally obtained the draft one day prior to the meeting after persistently requesting a copy from MORA, there was not much he could offer the public in terms of informed criticism.[173] Furthermore, Eri was astonished to receive a phone call inviting him to address a parliamentary discussion of the bill just one day prior to the meeting with legislative members on August 25, 1999. This procedure was unusual for such an important meeting. Eri was therefore convinced that MORA sought to dominate the enactment of this law without wide consultation, especially from those private institutions with a sound record in *zakat* administration.[174] This incident clearly shows that non-governmental elements were deliberately bypassed in the enactment of this law. Nevertheless, FOZ attempted to contribute some thoughts on certain provisions.[175]

Looking at the presentation of the bill to the DPR made by the minister of religion, it is clear that at least four reasons were behind the perceived need to enact *zakat* law in Indonesia: (1) the obsession to propose *zakat* as one of the resource funds that could be used for social welfare and poverty eradication, (2) the need to provide a stronger judicial foundation for *zakat* agencies in Indonesia, (3) the expectation that it would boost participation levels and could increase the amount of *zakat* payment from Muslims, and (4) the fact that there was no *zakat* agency at the national level.[176] Of these reasons, FOZ disagreed only with the last one.

The *zakat* bill appears to have been hastily drafted to meet triangular interests: to conform with *shariah*, satisfy Muslim constituents, and further the government's political interests. The first and second interests were evident from the wording of the law, but the last interest was more subtly veiled. Few would deny that by enacting laws such as this the Habibie government sought to attain broader political support from Muslims, especially in the lead up to the presidential elections.

At least two important issues arose during the legislative process that are related to the main argument of this study. First is the nature of *zakat* collection in Indonesia. The final draft of the bill prepared by MORA contained a provision initially drafted in Article 12, paragraph 1 that may be interpreted as imperative.

> '*Pengumpulan zakat dilakukan oleh badan amil zakat dengan cara menerima atau mengambil dari muzakki.*' [The collection of *zakat* is organized by the government-sponsored *zakat* agency responsible for receiving or taking *zakat* payment from the *zakat* payer.]

This provision, however, was criticized by the state secretary, who said that it implied coercion regarding *zakat* collection and would lead to the realization of the Jakarta Charter.[177] To assuage this criticism, the phrase "*atas dasar pemberitahuan muzakki*" was added to the end of the article and became:

> *Pengumpulan zakat dilakukan oleh badan amil zakat dengan cara menerima atau mengambil dari muzakki atas dasar pemberitahuan muzakki.* [The collection of *zakat* is organized by the government-sponsored *zakat* agency responsible for receiving or taking *zakat* payment from the *zakat* payer upon his confirmation.]

Although MORA had welcomed the change over the nature of *zakat* collection as suggested by the state secretary, there was a heated debate over Article 12, paragraph 1 when it was discussed at the Panitia Kerja (also known as Panja or Working Committee). During deliberations on the bill, Umar Shihab, a member of the Golkar faction (FKP, Fraksi Karya

Pembangunan), viewed the article as suggesting that the *zakat* agency be passive in collecting *zakat*. For Golkar, the *zakat* agency should be "proactive" in *zakat collection*. Therefore, FKP proposed that there must be a clause explaining this in the Elucidation of Law. This proposal might be seen as evidence of Golkar's leaning commitment towards Islamization during the 1990s. The FKP's proposal was criticized by the factions both of the Army (F-ABRI) and the Persatuan Pembangunan (FPP). Abdullah Hadi from F-ABRI contended that such a "proactive" proposal would create a reaction among the people, and that he believed it would have a fate similar to the taxation levied on televisions, which ended fruitlessly. Referring to the principles of *zakat* management, which are *iman and takwa* (faith and piety), mentioned in Article 4 of the bill, Abduh Paddare from FPP argued that the proactive *zakat* agency was not in line with this principle. According to him, the "*zakat* payers should have their own awareness to purify themselves and their wealth without coercion. Only then would they be rewarded by paradise in the hereafter."[178]

Responding to these criticisms, Shihab explained that what his faction meant by "proactive" was not coercion, but merely reminding (*mengingatkan*) Muslims to pay *zakat*. Citing a Qur'anic verse and a fragment from the history of early Islam, he differentiated between the phrases "to compel" and "to remind." Shihab further stated that his faction did not want to modify Article 12 but to give an explanation in the Elucidation of Law.[179] The proposal was eventually accepted not only because FKP had a great majority of representatives in the parliament, but also because other factions found the proposal would not change the voluntary nature of *zakat* payment. As a result, a new clause was created in the Elucidation of Law, Article 12, paragraph 1 stating, "*Dalam melaksanakan tugasnya, badan amil zakat harus bersikap proaktif melalui kegiatan komunikasi, informasi dan edukasi.*" [In undertaking its tasks, the *zakat* agency should be proactive through communication, information, and educational activities.] Although *zakat* payment was not made imperative, this new clause certainly became the basis for the campaign to popularize *zakat*.

The second issue that arose during the legislative process was the rivalry between BAZ and LAZ. The draft prepared by MORA was designed to provide BAZ with full legal arrangements and did not include LAZ in such arrangements. The formal administration of *zakat* would thus be centralized. However, there was strong criticism from LAZ, which was organized under FOZ. In fact, FOZ formed a special team led by Didin Hafiduddin to prepare its own draft.[180] Through this draft, they demanded that the existence of LAZ be acknowledged in the bill.

When DPR passed the bill, the existence of LAZ was finally mentioned, though its role was limited. In fact, out of the thirty-three articles mentioned in Decree No. 581/1999 that was issued as a detailed regulation by the minister of religious affairs, only four articles dealt with LAZ. It seemed that MORA did not want the bill to empower LAZ but rather to subordinate the organization into the lower structure of BAZ as a *zakat* collection unit (Unit Pengumpulan Zakat, UPZ). Later it appeared that the issue of the twin institutions of *zakat* administration (BAZ and LAZ) would be an obstacle in trying to centralize *zakat* collection.

Tax Deductibility of *Zakat* Payment

Muslims in Indonesia had long been waiting for *zakat* regulation. One aspect that they needed to see was a tax deduction for *zakat* payment. This was actually a long-held expectation of Muslims for avoiding the double burden of paying *zakat* and tax in the nation-state of Indonesia.[181] MORA sought to comply with this Muslim aspiration but felt it difficult to transform into legislation because it touched upon the jurisdiction of the Ministry of Finance. In response, MORA literally transferred the provision from the colonial regulation on social donation and taxation into the *zakat* bill.[182]

It should be noted that the Ministry of Finance had been involved in drafting the *zakat* bill since February 1999, but the extent to which the Ministry of Finance discussed tax deduction for *zakat* payment is not clear.

What is clear is that in May 1999, the Ministry of Finance sent a letter to MORA objecting to the provision. It was thought that such a provision would lessen the annual tax received by the Directorate of Taxation. In any case, there was no existing regulation on tax deductibility for *zakat* payments; although previous high officials had issued decrees on potential tax deductions for social donations.[183]

Due to a conflict of interest between the ministries, this problem was forwarded to the president to resolve.[184] President Habibie seemed not to welcome the Ministry of Finance's stance and therefore the essence of the provision remained untouched even until the bill was passed by DPR. The institutionalization of *zakat* to some extent had reached the point where the permeation of Islamic doctrine into the structure of a secular state began to deepen considerably and irreversibly. However, its actual implementation would not be more difficult.[185]

The complexity of implementing a tax deduction for *zakat* payments rests on the fact that full cooperation is required from both sanctioned *zakat* agencies and taxation offices at the local level—something not easily accomplished given that coordination between ministries at the national level does not run smoothly, as evidenced by the enactment of revised Law No. 17/2000 on income tax. When the draft of the revised income tax law was presented to DPR in May 2000, no provision supporting tax deductions for *zakat* payments had been included. It seemed that MORA was not involved at all in the discussion of the tax bill.

It is interesting to note here that, instead of MORA, it was FOZ that played a vital role in attempting to introduce the idea of a tax deduction for *zakat* payments into the revised tax law. When the income tax bill was being discussed in parliament, several FOZ activists met with Syamsul Balda, a legislator from the Justice Party (PK), and raised this issue. Through the *reformasi* faction, consisting of the National Mandate Party (PAN) and the Justice Party (PK), Balda criticized the bill for failing to allow *zakat* payments to become deductible from taxable net income. At the General Overview (*Pemandangan Umum*) of Factions of DPR, which was held on June 8, 2000, Balda suggested that such a provision be included in the bill. During the DPR meeting on June 14, 2000, the government (i.e., the minister of finance) finally welcomed Balda's suggestion and revised the bill to be in line with the *zakat* law provided, however, the proposed provision did not contradict the principles of income tax law.[186]

The actual application of a tax deduction for *zakat* payments has become increasingly complex. Although the *zakat* law was enacted in 2001, it took two years before it went into effect. *Muzakki (zakat* payers) had expected to receive a tax deduction by March 31, 2002 (the end of Indonesia's fiscal year 2001–2002), but this never occurred because no form was provided for itemizing *zakat* payments in the government's tax form packet (Surat Pemberitahuan Tahunan Pajak Penghasilan Wajib Pajak).[187]

In fiscal year 2003, *zakat* finally appeared on the government's tax form. Moreover, the Directorate of Taxation issued a decree with specific regulations on tax deductions for *zakat* payments. Nevertheless, tax deductibility remained an obstacle since the letter of proof of *zakat* payment (Bukti Setoran Zakat), as required by the Directorate of Taxation, was not yet available. The letter of proof form issued by BAZNAS lacked a line item for the total income of *muzakki*, including where and when they earned it, thereby causing further delay in achieving *zakat* tax deductions.[188] This demonstrates that as long as there is no coordination between related institutions, tax deductions for *zakat* payments remain on paper only.

There was a common belief that providing tax deductions for *zakat* payment would boost the amount of *zakat* funds from *muzakki*. However, this is an unrealistic expectation. The tax refund system in Indonesia does not apply the self-assessment principle. Consequently, few people would be encouraged to pay *zakat*, report its amount on the tax form, and apply for a tax deduction because tax officers would audit taxpayers' bookkeeping documents. If these documents were not audited, there would likely be tax corruption through *zakat* payment manipulation.[189] In light of this, it is hard to imagine that Indonesian Muslim businesses would really respond to this policy. Indeed, given the real problems with tax refunds in Indonesia, this policy is not likely to be successful in the short term. Perhaps attention should first be given to improving the efficiency of the tax refund system.

Instituting a *zakat* tax deduction has certainly not eliminated the double financial burden of Muslims living in the nation-state of Indonesia who are still required to pay both tax and *zakat*. Even though they may deduct 2.5 percent from their net taxable income, this is a small amount and has had little impact. Some Muslims in *zakat* agencies who were enthusiastic about having this policy included in both *zakat* and taxation laws are now disenchanted after seeing the real effect of this rule. They maintain that what they wanted was a tax credit (a reduction from the amount of tax charged), not a tax deduction as it is presently set up.[190]

With the introduction of this policy, a number of criticisms have arisen concerning religious discrimination. A *Jakarta Post* editorial fiercely questioned why the government had "singled out the Muslim community when it is well aware that followers of other creeds also pay religious donations."[191] Abdul Munir Mulkhan, a sociologist of religion at IAIN Yogyakarta, and Astrid Soesanto, a former legislative member from the Christian party (PDKB), strongly advocate the extension of the same policy to followers of other religions, since they also have sacred duties to make charitable donations.[192] However, the government could not immediately satisfy this demand. Said Agil Husein Al Munawar, minister of religious affairs in Megawati's government, noted that before the government would consider applying the tax-deductible *zakat* policy on similar kinds of almsgiving from other religions, it would first focus on *zakat* administration. In an attempt to reassure other religious groups, Al Munawar said, "God willing, we will arrange it later. . . . We will do this one by one."[193] It is thus clear that Islam has been given higher priority than other religions in Indonesian socio-political life over the past few years, thereby deepening the Islamization process.

AMENDMENTS TO THE *ZAKAT* LAW

The deepening of Islamization through regulating *zakat* practice became more noticeable with FOZ's efforts to amend the existing *zakat* law. In order to trace the trajectory of this Islamization, one must examine two concerns regarding the amendments to the *zakat* law: the demand that *zakat* evasion by rich Muslims be penalized and the expectation that the collection of *zakat* be centralized in the national board of *zakat* agencies, BAZNAS.

Amendments to the current *zakat* law arose on various occasions. The first took place at a public hearing (*dengar pendapat*) with parliamentary members on January 28, 2002. On this occasion, the DPR Commission of Six received a FOZ delegation consisting of Iskandar Zulkarnaen as the chief of delegation and seven other rank and file members. The meeting had only two agenda items: FOZ proposing its ideas for handling *zakat* administration and parliamentary members providing feedback.[194]

At this meeting, FOZ described the current conditions of *zakat* administration in Indonesia, citing at least seven problems that needed to be quickly resolved by the legislature: (1) the voluntary nature of *zakat* within the existing law means that the payment depends greatly on the religious awareness of wealthy Muslims; (2) since the current law contains no provisions for penalizing those who refuse to pay *zakat*, the role of the government is virtually absent from *zakat* administration; (3) anyone can establish a *zakat* agency; this situation has created unnecessary rivalries and inevitable conflicts between various agencies, especially between BAZ and LAZ; (4) as a result of the third problem, both the collection and distribution of *zakat* have been fragmented and less productive; (5) it is unclear which institution has the right to control and accredit a non-state *zakat* agency (LAZ); this situation seems to imply that the limits of jurisdiction between one LAZ and another have become blurred; (6) the position and role of BAZNAS as a national board of *zakat* agencies has remained unclear, and hence the establishment of a *zakat* collector unit (as a subordinate of BAZNAS) at a number of state-owned companies has been stagnant; and (7) the existing *zakat* law is not yet sufficient, for it lacks strong technical regulation at the lower levels. Indeed, according to FOZ, instead of a ministerial decree, a government regulation (*peraturan pemerintah*, PP) issued by the president should support this law.[195]

FOZ suggested, in a rather controversial move, that the current *zakat* law be amended in four areas. First, a new ministry, the Ministry of *Zakat* and *Wakaf* should be set up to manage the collection and distribution of *zakat* in Indonesia (Article 1). Second, the basis for this *zakat* management should be Islamic *shariah*, not Pancasila and the 1945 Constitution (Article 4). Third, *zakat* should no longer be based on the discretion of the *muzakki*, but rather collecting *zakat* should be an active task undertaken by a *zakat* agency or *amil* (Article 12). And, fourth, *zakat* should be mandatory for Muslims and anyone that evades paying *zakat* should be penalized (Additional Article).

FOZ emphasized the vital role of the state and requested that the government function optimally in undertaking *zakat* collection.[196] Many DPR members were wary of FOZ's proposal, especially the provision to change the voluntary nature of *zakat*. The proposed amendment was thus not widely welcomed.

Yet nearly all the *zakat* agencies supported the amendment proposal.[197] Not surprisingly, the Third National Congress of FOZ chose as its theme "Menggagas Amandemen UU no. 38 tahun 1999 tentang pengelolaan Zakat: Menuju Optimalisasi Dana Zakat" [Proposing the Idea of an Amendment to *Zakat* Law No. 38/1999: Towards Optimizing *Zakat* Funds]. Several non-government speakers, including Djamal Doa[198] and Sunarsip,[199] strongly advocated the urgency of the amendment, believing that centralizing *zakat* under state management and penalizing wealthy Muslims unwilling to pay *zakat* were vital to the optimization of *zakat* collection.[200] However, government speakers, such as Tulus[201] and Wahiduddin Adam,[202] preferred prioritizing consistent application of the current law and advocated strengthening the role of BAZNAS within existing regulations.[203]

At the FOZ congress, Adam critiqued the proposed amendment citing institutional, regulatory, human resource-related, and public awareness problems. In analyzing these, Adam wrote:

> Does one or all four problems above occur because of the nature of the regulation or due to its implementation? . . . If the problem has to do with regulation, is it created by the law itself or because of its lower technical policies? If it has to do with the regulation, would the amendment be a solution? How many provisions in the law need to be changed or replaced?[204]

For Adam, amending the *zakat* law is necessary only if there are strong reasons behind it.

> To prepare a bill or to amend a law we should pay careful attention to the motives that brought us to make or to change it; is it crucial or not, is it for a short-term goal or for a long-term objective. Do not manipulate the causes [for the amendment], which are not urgent and do not reflect reality, or are beyond the first priority . . . The effort to amend the law requires a basic urgency in terms of philosophical, juridical, and sociological aspects.[205]

Adam argued that regulatory problems were not the cause of the low level of *zakat* collection in Indonesia. Therefore, amending the law was not a solution. For Adam, it would be better to enhance people's trust of *zakat* agencies. He suggested that BAZ and LAZ needed to work harder in collecting and distributing *zakat* effectively. Adam was optimistic that if this approach worked well, employing an intimidating method (i.e., penalizing *zakat* evaders) would not be necessary or justifiable. Ultimately, people would make *zakat* payments sincerely and faithfully.

Although government officials within FOZ did not welcome the idea of the proposed amendment, changes to particular aspects of the *zakat* law were still proposed at the Third National Congress. These proposed changes appeared somewhat more lenient than the draft amendment presented at the public hearing with the DPR Commission of Six. For the most part, the majority raised no substantive issues with the changes proposed at the congress, except the terms of the penalty for wealthy Muslims who failed to pay *zakat*. It was now proposed that the penalty would be a year's imprisonment and a fine up to a twice of the total *zakat* amount due, excluding the obligatory *zakat* payment.[206]

Given that the congress still needed the elected chairman and his rank and file to continue drafting the amendment, FOZ Chairman Naharus Surur (2003–2006) formed a team to finalize the draft. This team was led by Teten Kustiawan (one of FOZ officials) and has been working for several years.[207] While it may be still too early to speculate whether FOZ will be successful in amending the *zakat* law, the clear signal is that—in light of Indonesia's current political environment where the Islamic parties did not win a majority of seats in the legislature following the 2004 election—their efforts will be fruitless.[208]

CONCLUSION

The Shift in *Zakat* Practice and Islamization

The shift in *zakat* practice in Indonesia began in the early years of the New Order regime and deepened only in the aftermath of the regime's collapse. The development of *zakat* administration in the early years of the New Order era underpinned this shift. During this period, the shift was minimal, almost dormant, though there was some progress, especially in terms of the willingness of the state to pay attention to Muslims' religious duties. It appears that the Ministry of Religious Affairs, as a sole player in facilitating *zakat* collection, needed a partner to accelerate the process of deepening *zakat* practice. In the early 1990s, as the political climate changed, Dompet Dhuafa Republika (DD) was established to benefit Muslims' interests in Indonesia. In 1997, the founding of FOZ (with DD as the leading institution during its early establishment) represented the catalyst MORA needed.

The structural shift in *zakat* practice began with the repercussions that ensued following the downfall of the Suharto government in 1998. The enactment of Law No. 38/1999 on *zakat* management marked a new day for the development of *zakat* practice in Indonesia. Through this law, the shift in *zakat* practice has become more deeply entrenched. Two aspects of the shift are once again worth mentioning here in relation to the process of Islamization in Indonesia. The first is BAZNAS. Its existence today as a part of the state structure and an institution under the authority of the Ministry of Religious Affairs is an important symbol that Islamization has intensified. The second aspect is the relationship between *zakat* and tax. Since this issue was dealt exclusively within the law, the intricate nexus between Muslim citizens' religious duties and the non-religious character of the modern nation-state seemed to be somewhat resolved, thus evidencing the fact that Islamization took place through the enactment of the *zakat* law.

There are also other cases where proponents of Islamization in Indonesia have sought to deepen the shift in *zakat* practice. One is the proposed amendment to the *zakat* law, which attempted to transform the nature of *zakat* practice from a voluntary to compulsory payment. The centralization of *zakat* collection as envisioned under the proposed amendment may be another example of the deepening shift in *zakat* practice, however, such centralization would put LAZ at a disadvantage and thus it is unlikely to attract much support.

With the implementation of regional autonomy that began in January 2001, a number of districts or municipalities have produced religious by-laws on *zakat* management. Through these constitutional means, whether nationally or locally, the state has made *zakat* something unavoidable, if not compulsory. The district of Balikpapan, East Kalimantan, for example, has begun allocating 2.5 percent of its *Pendapatan Asli Daerah* (PAD, Regional Basic Income) for *zakat* payment. This local "innovation" is considered an important step in intensifying the institutional shift in *zakat* practice.

A number of state-run and private-owned companies have asked their Muslim employees to perform the *zakat profesi* every month, in some cases making *zakat profesi* a professional obligation. *Zakat profesi* is a religious tax paid by professionals, such as civil servants, lawyers, doctors, and so forth. This kind of *zakat* is basically discretionary (the result of *ijtihad*), but is then made compulsory since it is considered parallel to income tax but with a 2.5 percent reduced charge from the net amount of the employee's wages.

Another example of the deepening shift in *zakat* practice is that, through the Ministry of Religious Affairs, BAZNAS requested the minister of finance to issue a regulation stipulating that all savings by Muslims deposited in an Indonesian bank are subject to *zakat*; that is for earning profit, i.e., interest from the bank. Although the minister of finance rejected BAZNAS's request, this represents a serious effort to boost the collection of *zakat* as well as to make it an obligatory payment.

In all of these examples of the deepening shift in *zakat* practice, FOZ was a leading player that not only met with parliamentary members but also organized seminars and conferences that advocated their issues.

The shift in *zakat* practice is still in progress and we do not know yet when it will be completed. In order to ascertain the future development of the shift, further studies are needed that look at the implications of the structural and institutional shifts as well as the cultural shift in *zakat* practice. The cultural shift should be viewed through the lens of to whom the *muzakki* pay their *zakat*, especially those who reside in townships and work as professionals. Do the *muzakki* alter the ways in which they make *zakat*—from personally and directly making contributions to individuals in society to now making contributions to a *zakat* agency? My inclination is to answer the question in the affirmative, especially if we consider that most of the *zakat* collected in Indonesia comes not from people who work on farms or in markets but from those working in offices (i.e., *zakat profesi*).[209]

Some surveys on *zakat* collection in Indonesia, such as those by PIRAC and PBB, have found that most Indonesian Muslims still pay their *zakat* in a traditional manner directly to the poor and not to a *zakat* agency. A study conducted by the Research Center of the Ministry of Religious Affairs also found the same thing. Based on these findings, the authors concluded that the enactment of the *zakat* law has not increased *zakat* collection in Indonesia. In my view, however, these research findings reveal a certain bias.

One needs to understand that the *zakat* law itself has not prevented people from paying their *zakat* directly to the poor and the needy. The *zakat* law exists to facilitate the official establishment of BAZ and LAZ, thus encouraging, not requiring, people to pay *zakat* to a *zakat* agency. Over eight years have passed since the law's enactment; yet it is still too early to conclude that the *zakat* law has been a failure merely based on the low national percentage (less than 25 percent) of Muslims paying *zakat* to BAZ or LAZ. Perhaps it would be fairer to measure the number of *muzakki* on BAZ's or LAZ's lists before and after the *zakat* law was enacted to determine whether the *muzakki* on those lists diverted their payment from poor people to *zakat* agencies. Only then would one be able to assess the success or failure of the current *zakat* law. This issue of a cultural shift in *zakat* practice, while pertinent, is beyond the scope of this study.

The rapid development of *zakat* in Indonesia became possible only during the third part of the twentieth century, when in the 1990s the New Order regime began lessening its pressure on political Islam. This development is not yet over and no one knows what its outcome will be. Two scenarios, which are not necessarily mutually exclusive, are possible. One scenario is that the current conditions of *zakat* collection, which are voluntary and decentralized, will serve as a preliminary entry point to the next stage in which the collection of *zakat* becomes compulsory and centralized (as in the Sudan case). The second scenario is that the practice of *zakat* will become so highly developed to meet worldly demands that it will eventually lose its authentic doctrine (as in the Pakistani case).

Unfortunately, the trajectory of current *zakat* practice in Indonesia seems to be following the latter model. This can be seen in certain provisions of *zakat* law that are subject to the provisions of taxation law. Indonesian Muslims have long assumed that by paying *zakat* they would be given a tax credit to avoid the double tax burden of being both citizens and religious adherents. However, what they have been granted so far is simply a tax deduction from net taxable income, in accordance with the provisions of taxation law. This state of affairs implies that Islamization in Indonesia does not necessarily represent the genuine application of Islamic doctrine. Thus, the enactment of the *zakat* law may not only be Islamizing Indonesia, but also Indonesianizing Islam.

NOTES

1   Christiaan Snouck Hurgronje, *Nasihat-Nasihat C. Snouck Hurgronje Semasa Kepegawaiannya Kepada Pemerintah Hindia Belanda 1880–1936*, vols. 1–7 (Jakarta: INIS, 1992). See esp. vol. 7, 1323–1379 on *zakat* and *fitrah*.

2   Sjechul Hadi Permono, *Pemerintah Republik Indonesia Sebagai Pengelola Zakat* (Jakarta: Pustaka Firdaus, 1993); H. M. Djamal Doa, *Menggagas Pengelolaan Zakat oleh Negara* (Jakarta: Nuansa Madani, 2001); Ahmad Sutarmadi, "Unifikasi dan Nasionalisasi Manajemen Pengelolaan Zakat Infak Shadaqah," paper presented at the national seminar on "Rekonseptualisasi Strategi Pendayagunaan Zakat untuk Pembangunan Ekonomi yang Berkeadilan dan Berkerakyatan untuk Menyongsong Abad 21," Faculty of Syariah IAIN Syarif Hidayatullah Jakarta, March 25–26, 1997.

3   Doa, *Menggagas Pengelolaan*; Eri Sudewo, "Mengkritisi UU Zakat," *Republika*, May 23, 2003.

4   Taufik Abdullah explained that the New Order's approach popularized the Islamic institution of *zakat* among Muslim citizens, and thus has indirectly led to the rising consciousness of Muslims about their *zakat* obligation. See Taufik Abdullah, "*Zakat* Collection and Distribution in Indonesia," in *The Islamic Voluntary Sector in Southeast Asia*, ed. Mohammed Ariff (Singapore: ISEAS, 1991), 50–84.

5   These eleven *zakat* agencies were Dompet Dhuafa Republika, BAZIS DKI Jakarta, Baitul Maal PT Pupuk Kujang, Baitul Maal PT Pupuk Kaltim, Baitul Maal Pertamina, Telkom Jakarta, Bapekis Bank Bumi Daya, LKS-Bank Muamalat Indonesia, Baperohis Hotel Indonesia, PT. Internusa Hasta Buana, and Sekolah Tinggi Ekonomi Indonesia (STEI) Jakarta.

6   See *Direktori Organisasi Pengelola Zakat di Indonesia* (Jakarta: FOZ, 2001), xi.

7   Sahri Muhammad, *Pengembangan Zakat dan Infak dalam Upaya Meningkatkan Kesejahteraan Masyarakat* (Malang: Yayasan Pusat Studi Avicena, 1982); Dawam Rahardjo, *Perspektif Deklarasi Makkah: Menuju Ekonomi Islam* (Bandung: Mizan, 1987); Sofwan Idris, *Gerakan Zakat dalam Pemberdayaan Ekonomi Umat:Pendekatan Transformatif* (Jakarta: Cita Putra Bangsa, 1997); Hidayat Syarief "Pendayagunaan Institusi Zakat sebagai Alternatif Pemberdayaan Ekonomi Rakyat," paper presented at the national seminar on "Rekonseptualisasi

Strategi Pendayagunaan Zakat untuk Pembangunan Ekonomi yang Berkeadilan dan Berkerakyatan untuk Menyongsong Abad 21," Faculty of Syariah IAIN Syarif Hidayatullah Jakarta, March 25–26, 1997; Didin Hafiduddin, *Zakat dalam Perekonomian Modern* (Jakarta: Gema Insani Press, 2002).

8   Syekhul Hadi Permono, "Pola Pemikiran Zakat Badan Amil Zakat, Infaq Shadaqah (BAZIS) DKI Jakarta" (master's thesis, IAIN Syarif Hidayatullah, Jakarta, 1984); Marzani Anwar, "BAZIS DKI Jakarta: Sosok Keamilan Modern," *Pesantren* 3, no. 2 (1986); Abdullah, "*Zakat* Collection."

9   Permono, *Pemerintah Republik*; Doa, *Menggagas Pengelolaan*.

10   Masdar F. Mas'udi, *Agama Keadilan: Risalah Zakat (Pajak) dalam Islam* (Jakarta: P3M, 1991).

11   Bahtiar Effendy, *Islam dan Negara: Transformasi Pemikiran dan Praktik Politik Islam di Indonesia* (Jakarta: Paramadina, 1998); Arskal Salim, "*Zakat* Administration in Politics of Indonesian New Order," in *Shari'a and Politics in Modern Indonesia*, eds. Arskal Salim and Azyumardi Azra (Singapore: ISEAS, 2003), 181–192.

12   Eri Sudewo, "Keterkaitan UU no. 38/1999 dengan UU no. 17/2000: Sebuah Pergeseran Paradigma," in *Problematika Zakat Kontemporer: Artikulasi Proses Sosial Politik Bangsa*, eds. Muhtar Sadili and Amru (Jakarta: FOZ, 2003), 11–25.

13   Harry J. Benda, *The Crescent and the Rising Sun: Indonesia Under the Japanese Occupation, 1942–1945* (The Hague/Bandung: W. van Hoeve Ltd., 1958); Merle C. Ricklefs, "Six Centuries of Islamization in Java," in *Conversion to Islam*, ed. N. Levtzion (New York: Holmes and Meir, 1979), 101–128; Azyumardi Azra, *Renaisans Islam Asia Tenggara: Sejarah Wacana dan Kekuasaan* (Bandung: Remaja Rosdakarya, 1999).

14   Ricklefs, "Six Centuries."

15   See, e.g., S. M. N. Al-Attas, *Preliminary Statement on a General Theory of Islamization of the Malay-Indonesian Archipelago* (Kuala Lumpur: Dewan Bahasa dan Pustaka, 1969); G. W. J. Drewes, "New Light on the Coming of Islam to Indonesia?," *Bijdragen tot de Taal-, Land-en Volkenkunde*, 124 (1968): 433–459.

16   See, e.g., Christian Pelras, "Religion, Tradition, and the Dynamics of Islamization in South Sulawesi," *Archipel* 29, no. 1 (1985): 107–135; J. Noorduyn, "Makasar and the Islamization of Bima", *Bijdragen tot de Taal-, Land-en Volkenkunde*, 143 (1987): 312–342.

17   See Clifford Geertz, *Islam Observed: Religious Development in Morocco and Indonesia* (Chicago: the University of Chicago, 1968); Mark R. Woodward, *Islam*

in Java: Normative Piety and Mysticism in Sultanate of Yogyakarta (Tucson: University of Arizona Press, 1989); A. C. Milner, "Islam and the Muslim State," in *Islam in South-East Asia,* ed. M. B. Hooker (Leiden: E. J. Brill, 1983), 23-49; G. W. J. Drewes, *An Early Javanese Code of Muslim Ethics* (The Hague: Martinus Nijhoff, 1978); M. B. Hooker, "The Translation of Islam into South-East Asia," in *Islam in South-East Asia,* ed. M. B. Hooker (Leiden: E. J. Brill, 1983); W. Cummings, "Scripting Islamization: Arabic Texts in Early Modern Makassar," *Ethnohistory* 48, no. 4 (2001): 559–586; Eldar Braten, "To Colour, Not Oppose: Spreading Islam in Rural Java," in *Muslim Diversity: Local Islam in Global Contexts,* ed. Leif Manger (Surrey: Curzon, 1999).

18   In Java, acculturated Islam became widespread by the end of the sixteenth century and prevailed, in part, due to the victory of Adiwijaya, the regent of Pajang, over Arya Penangsang, the regent of Jipang. The former subscribed to syncretic Javanese Islam, while the latter seemed to belong to orthodox Islam. See Kacung Marijan, "Islamization of Java: From Hindu-Buddhist Kingdoms to New Order Indonesia," *Jurnal Studi Indonesia* 8, no. 2 (1998): 6; G. Moejanto, *The Concept of Power in Javanese Culture* (Yogyakarta: Gadjah Mada University Press, 1990), 15. In West Sumatra, the Dutch intervention paved the way for *penghulu* (local *adat* figures) to succeed the Padri movement that wanted a comprehensive and radical reform of Islam. See Azra, *Jaringan Ulama,* 292.

19   Clifford Geertz, *The Religion of Java* (New York: The Free Press, 1960); C. Dobbin, *Islamic Revivalism in a Changing Peasant Economy: Central Sumatra, 1784–1847* (London: Curzon, 1983).

20   Ricklefs, "Six Centuries," 112–117.

21   Azra, *Jaringan Ulama,* 291–292.

22   Ricklefs, "Six Centuries," 101.

23   Ibid.

24   J. L. Peacock, *Purifying the Faith: The Muhammadiyah Movement in Indonesian Islam* (California: Cummings Publishing Company, 1978); H. M. Federspiel, *Persatuan Islam: Islamic Reform in Twentieth Century Indonesia* (Ithaca, NY: Cornell University, Modern Indonesia Project, 1970); Deliar Noer, *Gerakan Modern Islam di Indonesia 1900–1942* (Jakarta: LP3ES, 1980).

25   B. J. Boland, *The Struggle of Islam in Modern Indonesia* (The Hague: Martinus Nijhoff, 1982), 191.

26   Noer, *Gerakan Modern,* 241–254.

27   Chandra Muzaffar, "Islamisation of State and Society: Some Further Critical

Remarks," in *Shari'a Law and the Modern Nation-State*, ed. Norani Othman (Kuala Lumpur: Sisters in Islam, 1994), 113.

28   Ibid., 113–114.

29   Boland, *The Struggle of Islam*, 7–89, 144–156; Endang Saefuddin Anshari, *Piagam Jakarta 22 Juni 1945* (Jakarta: Rajawali Press, 1986); C. van Dijk, *Rebellion under the Banner of Islam: The Darul Islam in Indonesia* (The Hague: Martinus Nijhoff, 1981); *Syafi'i* Ma'arif, *Islam dan Masalah Kenegaraan: Studi Tentang Percaturan dalam Konstituante* (Jakarta: LP3ES, 1985); Adnan Buyung Nasution, *The Aspiration for Constitutional Government in Indonesia: A Socio-Legal Study of the Indonesian Konstituante 1956–1959* (Jakarta: Pustaka Sinar Harapan, 1992); Andi Faisal Bakti, *Islam and Nation Formation in Indonesia: From Communitarian to Organizational Communications* (Jakarta: Logos, 2000).

30   Muhammad Syukri Salleh, "Islamisation of State and Society: A Critical Comment," in *Shari'a Law and the Modern Nation-State*, ed. Norani Othman (Kuala Lumpur: Sisters in Islam, 1994), 108.

31   Martin Rossler, "Islamization and the Reshaping of Identities in Rural South Sulawesi," in *Islam in an Era of Nation-States: Politics and Religious Renewal in Muslim Southeast Asia*, eds. Robert W. Hefner and Patricia Horvatich (Honolulu: University of Hawai'i Press, 1997), 275–308.

32   See Robert W. Hefner, "Islamizing Capitalism: On the Founding of Indonesia's First Islamic Bank," in *Towards a New Paradigm: Recent Developments in Indonesian Islamic Thought*, eds. Mark Woodward and J. Rush (Tempe: Arizona State University Program in Southeast Asian Studies, 1995), 291–322.

33   Aware that political Islam could be eventually domesticated, the New Order regime began to treat it sympathetically by implementing a number of policies supposedly in line with Islamic socio-cultural and political interests, e.g., the passing of the Religious Courts law (1989), the founding of ICMI (1990), the compilation of Islamic laws (1991), the issuance of the joint ministerial decree on the guidance of the *zakat* collection board (BAZIS), the holding of an Islamic cultural festival (1991), the establishment of an Islamic Bank (1992), and the termination of the national lottery (1993). For further details on these political accommodations, see Effendy, *Islam dan Negara*.

34   See, e.g., Robert W. Hefner, "Islamizing Java? Religion and Politics in Rural East Java," *The Journal of Asian Studies* 46, no. 3 (1987): 533–554; Abdul Azis Thaba, *Islam dan Negara dalam Politik Orde Baru* (Jakarta: Gema Insani Press, 1996); Aminuddin, *Kekuatan Islam dan Pergulatan Kekuasaan di Indonesia: Sebelum dan Sesudah Runtuhnya Rezim Soeharto* (Yogyakarta: Pustaka Pelajar, 1999); M.

Rusli Karim, *Negara dan Peminggiran Islam Politik* (Yogyakarta: Tiara Wacana, 1999); O. Farouk Bajunid, "Islam and State in Southeast Asia", in *State and Islam*, eds. C. van Dijk and A. H. de Groot (Leiden: Research School CNWS, 1995).

35 Boland, *The Struggle of Islam*, 164, 192–204. Having failed to reestablish the Masyumi political party, which was previously banned by Sukarno in 1960, one of its prominent leaders, Mohammad Natsir, in 1967 decided to devote himself to *dakwah* (Islamic preaching) rather than politics by founding the Dewan Dakwah Islamiyah Indonesia (DDII, the Council of Islamic Propagation of Indonesia). This council has sought to transform Indonesians into more pious Muslims since it believes that the negative responses toward the implementation of *shariah* through the Jakarta Charter during the Constituent Assembly period (1957–1959) were a clear sign that further Islamization of society is needed. See Martin van Bruinessen, "Genealogies of Islamic Radicalism in Post-Suharto Indonesia," *South East Asia Research* 10, no. 2 (July 2002): 117–154.

36 Arskal Salim, "Shari'a in Indonesia's Current Transition: An Update," in *Shari'a and Politics of Modern Indonesia*, eds. Arskal Salim and Azyumardi Azra (Singapore: ISEAS, 2003), 213–232.

37 Ali Said Damanik, *Fenomena Partai Keadilan: Transformasi 20 Tahun Gerakan Tarbiyah di Indonesia* (Jakarta: Teraju, 2002); Irfan S. Awwas, ed., *Risalah Kongres Mujahidin I dan Penegakan Syari'ah Islam* (Yogyakarta: Wihdah Press, 2001); Habib M. Rizieq Syihab, *Dialog Piagam Jakarta: Kumpulan Jawaban* (Jakarta: Pustaka Ibnu Sidah, 2000); Khamami Zada, *Islam Radikal: Pergulatan Ormas-Ormas Islam Garis Keras di Indonesia* (Jakarta: Teraju, 2002).

38 For a discussion on Islamization in these Muslim countries, see Ann Elizabeth Mayer, "The Fundamentalist Impact on Law, Politics and Constitutions in Iran, Pakistan and the Sudan," in *Fundamentalism and The State: Remaking Polities, Economies and Militance*, eds. Martin E. Marty and R. Scott Appleby (Chicago and London: University of Chicago Press, 1993), 110–151; Ann Elizabeth Mayer, "Law and Religion in Muslim Middle East," *The American Journal of Comparative Law* 35 (1987): 127–184.

39 Those entitled to receive *zakat* are listed in Q.S. 9:60: "The alms are only for the poor and the needy, and those who collect them, and those whose hearts are to be reconciled, and to free the captives and the debtors, and the cause of Allah, and (for) the wayfarers: a duty imposed by Allah. Allah is All-knowing, Wise."

40 For further detail, see Farishta G. de Zayas, *The Law and Philosophy of Zakat: the Islamic Social Welfare System* (Damascus: al-Jadidah Printing Press, 1960); Abdul Rehman Ansari, *Zakat: the Religious Tax of Islam* (Durban, South

Africa: Premier Press, 1973); Mahmoud Abu-Saud, *Fiqh Al-Zakat Al-Mu'asir* (East Burnham, Bucks, UK: Oxford Publishing, 1989).

41   See Jamal Malik, *Colonialization of Islam: Dissolution of Traditional Institutions in Pakistan* (New Delhi: Manohar, 1996), 85.

42   Timur Kuran, "Islamic Redistribution through Zakat: Historical Record and Modern Realities," in *Poverty and Charity in Middle Eastern Contexts,* eds. Michael Bonner, Mine Ener, and Amy Singer (Albany: State University of New York Press, 2002), 277.

43   A recent study conducted in rural Egypt shows that while 96 percent of farmers were aware of the obligatory *zakat* payment, only 20 percent of them paid *zakat* on their crops. See A. T. Abu Kuraysha, *Al-Zakat wa al-Tanmiya* (Cairo, 1999), cited in A. Zysow, "Zakat," *The Encylopaedia of Islam,* New Edition, vol. 11, (2002), 420.

44   Kuran, "Islamic Redistribution," 275–276.

45   Q.S. 9:60. See note 39.

46   Q.S. 9:103. "Take alms of their wealth, wherewith you may purify them and may make them grow."

47   See Suliman Bashear, "On the Origins and Development of the Meaning of *Zakat* in Early Islam," *Arabica* 40 (1993): 84–113.

48   The practice of *zakat* is spiritual in the sense that by giving *zakat* the remainder of one's wealth is purified as well as one's soul through restraining greed and imperviousness to others' sufferings. The recipient of *zakat,* likewise, is purified from jealousy and hatred of the well-off. See Jonathan Benthall, "Financial Worship: The Qur'anic Injunction to Almsgiving," *Journal of the Royal Anthropological Institute* 5 (March 1999): 29–30; Zakiah Daradjat, *Zakat: Pembersih Harta Dan Jiwa* (Jakarta: YPI Ruhana, 1991).

49   The practice of *zakat* is political in that *zakat* in the first centuries of Islam was designed to raise revenue for the Islamic state, allowing the state to spend *zakat* revenue on public works and territorial expansion. See Timur Kuran, "The Economic Impact of Islamic Fundamentalism," in *Fundamentalisms and the State: Remaking Polities, Economies and Militance,* eds. M. Marty and S. Appleby (Chicago: University of Chicago Press, 1993), 318.

50   *Zakat's* economic goals are to reduce poverty and inequality. See Josep-Antoni Ybarra, "The Zaqat in Muslim Society: an Analysis of Islamic Economic Policy," *Social Science Information* 35 (1996): 643–656; see also Idris, *Gerakan Zakat.*

51   See Benthall, "Financial Worship," 29; Zysow, "Zakat," 420.

52 Zysow, "Zakat," 418–419.

53 Ibid., 419.

54 See, e.g., Ann Elizabeth Mayer, "Islamization and Taxation in Pakistan," in *Islamic Reassertion in Pakistan: The Application of Islamic Laws in a Modern State*, ed. Anita M. Weiss (Syracuse: Syracuse University Press, 1986), 59–77; Grace Clark, "Pakistan's Zakat and 'Ushr as a Welfare System," in *Islamic Reassertion*, 79–95; Dimitri B. Novossyolov, "The Islamization of Welfare in Pakistan," in *Russia's Muslim Frontiers: New Directions in Cross-Cultural Analysis*, ed. Dale F. Eickelman (Bloomington and Indianapolis: Indiana University Press, 1993), 160–174; Malik, *Colonialization of Islam*, esp. chapter 4 on the *zakat* system, 85–119; Gilles Kepel, *Jihad: The Trail of Political Islam*, trans. Anthony F. Roberts (Cambridge, Massachusetts: The Belknap Press of Harvard University Press, 2002), 98–105.

55 The practice of *zakat* in Pakistan has redistributed funds from those better off to those worse off, and so achieves some reduction in measured income inequality. However, the amount of change is generally minimal. See Geoffrey A. Jehle, "Zakat and Inequality: Some Evidence from Pakistan," *The Review of Income and Wealth* 40 (June 1994): 205–216; cf. Clark, "Pakistan's Zakat," 93–94.

56 Kepel, *Jihad: The Trail*, 102.

57 Novossyolov, "The Islamization of Welfare," 160.

58 Mayer, "Islamization and Taxation," 71–72.

59 Ibid., 72.

60 Ibid. However, as Kepel has noted, this exemption caused indignation among the more conservative Sunni *ulama*, who were afraid that a great amount of Pakistani Sunni Muslims would convert to Shia for the purpose of *zakat* evasion. See Kepel, *Jihad: The Trail*, 102.

61 Mayer, "Islamization and Taxation," 73.

62 Ibid., 62.

63 Ibid., 64.

64 Ibid., 71. *Zakat* evasion was also observable in Kedah, Malaysia during the period 1968–1978. In this case, the pattern of evasion was simply the reluctance of some farmers to pay *zakat* for various reasons. For further details, see James C. Scott, "Resistance Without Protest and Without Organization: Peasant Opposition to the Islamic Zakat and the Christian Tithe," *Comparative Studies in Society and History* 29 (July 1987): 417–452.

65 Malik, *Colonialization of Islam*, 104–105.

66 Novossyolov, "The Islamization of Welfare," 168–171.

67 These letters were compiled and edited by E. Gobee and C. Adriannse in *Ambtelijk Adviezen van C. Snouck Hurgronje 1889–1936* ('s-Gravenhage: Martinus Nijhoff, 1957). See esp. vol. 2, chapter 28 on *djakat en pitrah*. I am referring here to its Indonesian version translated by Sukarsi and cited in note 1; hereafter referred to as *Nasihat-Nasihat*.

68 Karel Steenbrink, *Beberapa Aspek Tentang Islam di Indonesia Abad ke-19* (Jakarta: Bulan Bintang, 1984), 227–228; Abdullah, "Zakat Collection," 57; Muhammad Hisyam, *Caught Between Three Fires: The Javanese Pangulu Under the Dutch Colonial Administration 1882–1942* (Jakarta: INIS, 2001), 111–120.

69 Aqib Suminto, *Politik Islam Hindia Belanda* (Jakarta: LP3ES, 1985). Suminto discusses *zakat* only cursorily under the issue of mosque funds; although he does provide great detail on Dutch Islamic policy, which he believes was basically formulated to accommodate religious worship and Islamic family matters, but to reject any aspects of political Islam that might pose a threat to colonial rule.

70 Cf. Merle Ricklefs, *History of Modern Indonesia since c. 1200* (Stanford, California: Stanford University Press, 2001), 36–58. It should be noted, however, that there were some Arabs and other foreign individuals who served in the local sultanate.

71 *Nasihat-Nasihat*, 1324–1325.

72 Ibid., 1325.

73 In the Sultanate Banten during the sixteenth to seventeenth century, Pakih Najamuddin exercised this kind of judicial and political power. For further discussion, see Martin van Bruinessen, "Shari'a Court, Tarekat and Pesantren: Religious Administration in the Banten Sultanate," *Archipel* 50 (1995): 166–199.

74 *Nasihat-Nasihat*, 1325.

75 G. P. Rouffaer, "Vorstenlanden," *Adatrechtbundels*, vol. 34, *Java en Madoera* ('s-Gravenhage: Martinus Nijhoof, 1931), 309. I thank Merle Ricklefs for pointing out this particular piece and translating it from the Dutch for me.

76 *Nasihat-Nasihat*, 1325, 1347; Hisyam, *Caught Between*, 117; see also Karel A. Steenbrink, *Beberapa Aspek Tentang Islam di Indonesia Abad ke-19* (Jakarta: Bulan Bintang, 1984), 227–228.

77 *Nasihat-Nasihat*, 1335–1336; Hisyam, *Caught Between*, 117.

78 *Nasihat-Nasihat*, 1347, 1369, 1371.

79 Ibid., 1364, 1376; Steenbrink, *Beberapa Aspek*, 230.

80 This vow was conveyed when the reorganization of the Priangan residency was being planned. The commissioner was afraid that religious officials would oppose the reorganization plan, if it affected the existing practice of *zakat* collection in that region. See *Nasihat-Nasihat,* 1348–1349.

81 Ibid., 1330–1331; Abdullah, *Zakat Collection,* 57. In some cases, a small share of *zakat* was handed over to Muslim students (*santri*), the needy, and even sometimes to newly converted Muslims (*mu'allaf*).

82 *Nasihat-Nasihat,* 1368–1370.

83 Ibid., 1335.

84 One such threat was: "If you do not pay me *zakat,* I will not be responsible for your funeral rites or those of your family, or assist when you marry." See Hisyam, *Caught Between,* 117.

85 *Nasihat-Nasihat,* 1355.

86 Ibid., 1323, 1348, 1359.

87 Suminto, *Politik Islam,* 13–14. As Suminto points out, Snouck Hurgronje thought that religious piety in Islam "such as praying five times daily, fasting during the month of Ramadan [and may be the annual payment of *zakat* as well] was a heavy burden for Muslims living in the current period of the twentieth century. These heavy burdens gradually would cause Muslims to ignore the observance of their strict and conservative religious obligations." In Snouck Hurgronje's view, any intervention to prohibit the observance of such religious obligations would only inhibit the gradual abandonment of religious practices.

88 *Nasihat-Nasihat,* 1346–1354.

89 Ibid., 1352.

90 Ibid., 1360.

91 Ibid., 1374–1375.

92 Harry J. Benda, "Christiaan Snouck Hurgronje and the Foundations of Dutch Islamic Policy in Indonesia," *The Journal of Modern History* 30 (December 1958): 342.

93 Ibid., 341.

94 See Sayuti Thalib, *Receptio in Contrario* (Jakarta: Bina Aksara, 1982).

95 See *Nasihat-Nasihat,* 1348.

96 Ibid., 1377.

97 Ibid.

98   Ibid., 1358–1359.

99   Ibid., 1351.

100 Suminto, *Politik Islam*, 29–30. Suminto noted that Dutch colonial personnel maintained constant oversight of the religious courts, marriage and divorce, education, mosque funds, and pilgrimages to Mecca.

101 Nasihat-Nasihat, 1323–1324, 1350.

102 Ibid., 1349.

103 See Benda, *The Crescent and the Rising Sun*, 144–149; cf. Abdullah, "Zakat Collection," 57–58.

104 See Article 6 and 7 of Law No. 38/1999 on *zakat* management.

105 Boland, *The Struggle of Islam*, 9–10.

106 Andi Lolo Tonang, "Beberapa Pemikiran tentang Mekanisme Badan Amil Zakat," in *Zakat dan Pajak*, ed. B. Wiwoho (Jakarta: PT Bina Rena Pariwara, 1992), 262.

107 Boland, *The Struggle of Islam*, 159.

108 See Minister of Religion Mohammad Dachlan, "Piagam Djakarta Sumber Hukum Mendjiwai U.U.D. 1945," *Kiblat*, 3–4, no. 16 (1968).

109 NU figures who became ministers for religious affairs in the early years of the New Order era were Kiai Haji Saefuddin Zuhri and Kiai Haji Mohammad Dachlan. See Azyumardi Azra and Saiful Umam, eds., *Menteri-Menteri Agama RI: Biografi Sosial Politik* (Jakarta: INIS-PPIM-Balitbang Depag RI, 1998).

110 See Masykuri Abdillah, *Responses of Indonesian Muslim Intellectuals to the Concept of Democracy* (Hamburg: Abera Network Austronesia, 1997), 50; cf. Andree Feillard, NU *vis-à-vis Negara: Pencarian Isi, Bentuk dan Makna*, trans. from *Islam et Armee Dans L'Indonesie Contemporaine Les Pionners de la tradition* (Yogjakarta: LKIS, 1995), 135.

111 Feillard, NU *vis-à-vis Negara*, 140.

112 Tonang, "Beberapa Pemikiran," 264.

113 See Suharto's speech delivered at the Isra' Mi'raj (Prophet's Ascension) Celebration on October 26, 1968. The full text of his speech can be found in *Pedoman Zakat* (Jakarta: Proyek Pembinaan Zakat dan Wakaf, 1992/1993), 403–409.

114 Presidential Decree No. 07/PRIN/10/1968, dated October 31, 1968. The three military officers assigned to the nationwide *zakat* collection drive were Major-General Alamsyah, Colonel Azwar Hamid, and Colonel Ali Afandi. See Abdullah, "Zakat Collection," 51.

115 Presidential Letter No. B. 133/PRES/11/1969, dated November 28, 1968. It is worth noting here that on December 5, 1968, a week after this presidential letter was issued, the Governor of the Capital Special Region of Jakarta Ali Sadikin issued a decree regarding the founding of the *zakat* agency Badan Amil Zakat. Although the governor's decree referenced various higher regulations (such as those by the minister of religious affairs as well as President Suharto's official speech), one may safely speculate that Suharto's scheme to co-opt the institution of *zakat* by personally taking responsibility for collecting and distributing *zakat* had the most impact on the governor's decree. This is because the upshot of the cooptation of *zakat* collection by President Suharto was twofold: (1) *zakat* should be deposited into the president's account and not into MORA's *Baitul Maal* (Islamic Treasuries), and (2) the establishment of provincial *zakat* agencies was based on the governor's policy or his instruction and not because of MORA's regulation.

116 Salim, "Zakat Administration," 185.

117 Abdullah, "Zakat Collection," p. 69.

118 Muslim civil servants under the organization of KORPRI (Corps of Indonesian State Employees) were required to contribute alms (*sedekah*) ranging from fifty to one thousand rupiahs per person depending on their employment strata. By 1991, YABMP had raised over US$80 million and built more than 400 mosques. See Effendy, *Islam dan Negara*, 305.

119 Abdullah, "Zakat Collection," 60.

120 Ibid., 61.

121 According to PIRAC's research findings in eleven cities across Indonesia, 66 percent of *muzakkis* pay *zakat* to the local committee close to their home and 28 percent give *zakat* payment directly to eligible recipients. See *Pola Kecenderungan Masyarakat Berzakat* (Jakarta: PIRAC, 2002), 17–18.

122 See Effendy, *Islam dan Negara*, 300. This was due to the fact that many bureaucrats at the Ministry of Internal Affairs as well as the cabinet secretary regarded the involvement of government entities as a step towards implementing the Jakarta Charter, a controversial phrase that requires *shariah* to be formally applied.

123 On one occasion in 1991, Munawir Sjadzali (minister of religious affairs) and K. H. Hasan Basri (chairman of the Indonesian Council of Ulama) consulted with President Suharto. Both requested that the president issue a presidential decree (Keppres) or a presidential instruction (Inpres) on *zakat* management and asked if Suharto would again act as an official national *amil*. Suharto refused this request, saying it would be better for *zakat* to be administered by the two ministers in

a joint decree, and leave it to Muslims themselves to manage *zakat*. In this way, Muslims voluntarily perform *zakat*, while the government facilitates its operation. See *Pedoman Pembinaan BAZIS: Hasil Pertemuan Nasional I BAZIS se-Indonesia tanggal 3–4 Maret 1992* (Jakarta: Dirjen Bimas Islam Urusan Haji Departemen Agama, 1992), 79, 83.

124 The full text of these joint ministerial decrees and ministerial instructions can be found in Fadlullah, *Mengenal Hukum ZIS*, 260–263, 316–323. See also *Pedoman Pembinaan*, 116–131.

125 Interview with Mukhtar Zarkasyi (former director of Islamic affairs for MORA, 1990–1993), Jakarta, September 11, 2003. The former Minister of Religion Munawir Sjadzali told the audience at the national meeting of BAZIS that he would invite Rudini, the former minister of internal affairs, to participate in forming a National Coordination Board of BAZIS. It seemed, however, that President Suharto did not approve of the idea.

126 Several studies have revealed that Suharto's policy on Islam followed Snouck Hurgronje's advice on Islamic affairs. See, e.g., W. F. Wertheim, *Indonesie van Vorstenrijk tot Neokolonie*, cited in Karel Steenbrink, *Dutch Colonialism and Indonesian Islam: Contacts and Conflicts 1596–1950* (Amsterdam and Atlanta, Georgia: Rodopi B.V., 1993), 145.

127 Wiwoho (ed.), *Zakat and Pajak*, 277–292.

128 Masdar F. Mas'udi, *Agama Keadilan: Risalah Zakat (Pajak) dalam Islam* (Jakarta: P3M, 1991), xiii.

129 Ibid., 113–125.

130 Masdar F. Mas'udi, "Zakat: an Ethical Concept of Taxation and State: A Reinterpretation of Third Pillar of Islam," unpublished paper, n.d., 19–20.

131 Interview with Masdar F. Mas'udi, Jakarta, August 25, 2003.

132 See Mas'udi, "Zakat: an Ethical Concept," 20.

133 Ibid., 18.

134 Ibid., 21.

135 Interview with Masdar F. Mas'udi, Jakarta, August 19, 1999.

136 Dawam Rahardjo, "Manajemen Zakat," in *Pedoman Pembinaan BAZIS: Hasil Pertemuan Nasional I BAZIS Se-Indonesia tanggal 3–4 Maret 1992* (Jakarta: Bimas Islam dan Urusan Haji, 1992), 25.

137 Ibid., 25; interview with Dawam Rahardjo, Jakarta, August 28, 2003.

138 See Ministerial Decree No. KEP.650/MK/11/5/1976 issued by the Minister of

Finance Ali Wardhana and Circular Letter No. SE-11/PJ.62/1979 signed by the General Director of Taxation Sutadi Sukarya.

139 Law No. 38/1999, Art. 14 on *zakat* management states, "Zakat yang telah dibayarkan kepada badan amil zakat atau lembaga amil zakat dikurangkan dari laba/pendapatan sisa kena pajak dari wajib pajak yang bersangkutan sesuai dengan peraturan perundang-undangan yang berlaku." [*Zakat* that has been paid to the official agency is deducted from the rest of the taxable profit or income of the tax payer according to the applicable regulations.]

140 Law No. 17/2000, Art. 9 on income tax states, "Bahwa untuk menentukan besarnya penghasilan kena pajak bagi wajib pajak dalam negeri dan bentuk usaha tetap, tidak boleh dikurangkan oleh; . . . kecuali zakat atas penghasilan yang nyata-nyata dibayarkan oleh wajib pajak orang pribadi pemeluk agama Islam dan atau wajib pajak badan dalam negeri yang dimiliki oleh pemeluk agama Islam kepada badan amil zakat atau lembaga amil zakat yang dibentuk atau disahkan oleh pemerintah" [In order to estimate the amount of taxable income of resident taxpayers or enterprises, one is not allowed to deduct; . . . except *zakat* on income that is correctly paid by Muslim individuals or indigenous companies owned by Muslims to the official *zakat* agencies].

141 The eleven founding institutions of Forum Zakat are (1) Dompet Dhuafa Republika, (2) BAZIS DKI Jakarta, (3) Baitul Maal Pupuk Kujang, (4) Baitul Maal Pupuk Kaltim, (5) BAZIS Pertamina, (6) BDI PT Telkom, (7) Bapekis Bank Bumi Daya, (8) LKS Bank Muamalat Indonesia, (9) Baperohis Hotel Indonesia, (10) PT Internusa Hasta Buana, and (11) Sekolah Tinggi Ekonomi Indonesia.

142 Eri Sudewo was an employee at the daily paper *Republika*. He then founded Dompet Dhuafa Republika (DD) in 1993. He was the first chairman of FOZ (January–December 1999).

143 Abdul Shomad Muin was a former chairman of BAZIS DKI Jakarta (1996–2001).

144 Hilman was a former vice chairman of BAZIS DKI Jakarta (1996–2001). He was a close partner of Abdul Shomad Muin.

145 Aminuddin Daim was an employee of PT Pupuk Kujang who was involved in FOZ since its early beginnings.

146 Hadi Tjahyono is an employee of PT Pertamina who was involved in FOZ since its early beginnings.

147 Iskandar Zulkarnaen is director of PT Internusa Hasta Buana. He was the second chairman of FOZ (2000–2003).

148 Ismail Yusanto is a spokesperson of Hizbut Tahrir Indonesia. He was a former secretary general of FOZ (2000–2003).

149 Agus Sarwanto was a head of the secretariat during the early period of Iskandar Zulkarnaen's leadership. He resigned from the job in 2000 and chose to pursue his career through other employment.

150 This diagram comes from Iskandar Zulkarnaen, "Pentingnya Jaringan Kerja Antar Lembaga Pengelola Zakat untuk Mengatasi Problematika Ummat," paper presented at Semiloka Dai dan Muballigh Se-Jabotabek, March 1, 2003, 10.

151 See Decree of Minister of Religion No. 373/2003, Article 22 on the implementation of Law No. 38/1999 on *zakat* management.

152 The sixteen accredited LAZ are:
1. LAZ Dompet Dhuafa Republika
2. LAZ Yayasan Amanah Takaful
3. LAZ Pos Keadilan Peduli Umat
4. LAZIS Muhammadiyah
5. LAZ Yayasan Baitul Maal Muamalat
6. LAZ Yayasan Baitul Maal Hidayatullah
7. LAZ Yayasan Dana Sosial Al Falah
8. LAZ Persatuan Islam (Persis)
9. LAZ Yayasan Bamuis Bank BNI
10. LAZ Yayasan Bangun Sejahtera Mitra Umat
11. LAZ Dewan Dakwah Islamiyah Indonesia
12. LAZ Baitulmaal Bank BRI
13. LAZ Baitulmal wat Tamwil
14. LAZ Dompet Sosial Ummul Quro (DSUQ)
15. LAZ Baituzzakah Pertamina (BAZMA)
16. LAZ Darut Tauhid Bandung

This list was compiled from *Direktori Lembaga Amil Zakat* (Jakarta: Direktorat Pengembangan Zakat dan Wakaf, 2003) and an interview with Isbir Fadly, Jakarta, October 26, 2004.

153 Interview with a former FOZ activist, Jakarta, May 20, 2004.

154 For further details, see herein "The Structural Shift in *Zakat* Practice."

155 See *Hasil Rumusan Musyawarah Kerja Nasional I Lembaga Pengelola ZIS*, (Jakarta: FOZ, 1999), 7–8.

156 See *Hasil Rumusan Musyawarah Nasional III Forum Zakat: Menggagas Amandemen UU no. 38 tahun 1999 tentang Pengelolaan Zakat, Menuju Optimalisasi Dana Zakat*, Balikpapan (April 25–28, 2003), 24.

157 For further discussion, see herein "Amendments to the *Zakat* Law."

158 For further detail on PKPU, see *Direktori Organisasi Pengelola Zakat di Indonesia* (Jakarta: FOZ, 2001), 113–116; http://www.pkpu.or.id.

159 For further detail on PKS, see Ali Said Damanik, *Fenomena Partai Keadilan: Transformasi 20 Tahun Gerakan Tarbiyah di Indonesia* (Jakarta: Teraju, 2002).

160 See *Laporan Evaluasi Satu Tahun Kepengurusan Forum Zakat 1424 H* (Jakarta: FOZ, 2004), 9. It is regrettable that the dialogue, which was attended by representatives from several political parties, did not address the issue of amending the *zakat* law.

161 *Republika*, March 4, 2004.

162 Law No. 38/1999. This law is more about *zakat* management than the rules of *zakat* itself. However, the law is referred to herein as *zakat* law, simply to avoid using complicated terms.

163 Due to strong resistance from non-state *zakat* agencies (LAZ), the law eventually acknowledged their position. This situation inevitably retarded the shift in *zakat* practice because the law considers BAZ and LAZ to have equal status and similar tasks in managing *zakat*. The diversification of *zakat* agencies in Indonesia certainly diffuses *zakat* collection in many hands, thus creating difficulties for centralizing *zakat* collection. Lately, an awareness has emerged that these twin institutions of *zakat* management are not appropriate for maximizing the collection of *zakat*.

164 This information comes from a speech by Ahmad Sutarmadi delivered at a seminar I attended on the "Dissemination of the Bill on *Zakat* Laws," Treva Hotel, Jakarta, August 19, 1999.

165 Majelis Ulama Indonesia (MUI), the minister of religion, and eleven provincial *zakat* agencies (West Java, North Sumatra, East Java, West Kalimantan, South Sulawesi, West Sumatra, East Kalimantan, Yogyakarta, Central Kalimantan, Central Java, and North Sulawesi) supported the idea of a national *zakat* board. See *Pedoman Pembinaan*, 90–104.

166 This type of expression is common in the Indonesian context; it is used to indirectly convey the speaker's unwillingness to accept a request made to him. For the full text of Rudini's remarks, see *Pedoman Pembinaan*, 87.

167 Wahiduddin Adam pointed out three reasons why this proposal was rejected: (1) under the Jakarta Charter, the involvement of state officials would be considered a state intervention in religious affairs; (2) given people's lack of trust in the state's commitment, there was no consensus on whether to centralize the collection of

zakat; and (3) many people still regarded *zakat* payment as traditional income for organizing Islamic schools, private foundations, and *dakwah* (Islamic preachings). See "Amandemen Undang-Undang nomor 38 tahun 1999 tentang Pengelolaan Zakat: Dalam Perspektif Hukum," in *Hasil Rumusan Musyawarah Nasional III*, 88.

168 The *zakat* bill had been drafted since February 1999 under a team formed by MORA that included representatives of institutions such as the Department of Justice, Department of Finance, MUI, universities, and FOZ as well as several parliamentary members. Interview with Mukhtar Zarkasyi, Jakarta, September 11, 2003; interview with Miftahul Munir (former head of sub-directorate of *zakat* and *wakaf*, MORA), Jakarta, August 27, 2003.

169 The last day of the Bamus (Badan Musyawarah) meeting of DPR members was the same day that the *zakat* bill was sent to DPR. Although, the DPR didn't receive the bill until the following day. This made the bill ineligible for discussion because several parliamentary members' terms in office were expiring and they would be replaced by new members who had won seats in the 1999 election. The general secretary of DPR therefore sent the bill back to the state secretary saying that it should be delivered to the new DPR members who would be inaugurated in October 1999. Mukhtar Zarkasyi, the then head of the Legal Bureau and Public Relations of MORA who understood the situation, approached the PPP faction at DPR (Zarkasih Noor) in order to initiate a reopening of the Bamus meeting. Mukhtar was successful and the Bamus meeting was reconvened on July 26, 2003 with one agenda item only—the presentation of the *zakat* bill by the minister of religion. Interview with Mukhtar Zarkasyi, Jakarta, September 11, 2003.

170 Masdar F. Mas'udi, director of Perhimpunan Pengembangan Pesantren dan Masyarakat (P3M), is popular for his controversial book on *zakat* issues. In his work, entitled *Risalah Zakat (Pajak)*, Masdar argues that *zakat* and tax are indistinguishable according to Islamic doctrine.

171 Eri Sudewo, chairman of Forum Zakat (FOZ), is well known for his efforts to collect and distribute *zakat* through the Dompet Dhuafa Institute, an organization that works to economically empower lower income Muslims in Indonesia.

172 This information comes from a speech by Masdar F. Mas'udi delivered at the seminar "Dissemination of the Bill of Zakat Laws," Treva Hotel, Jakarta, August 19, 1999.

173 Eri Sudewo, "Ahlan Wa Sahlan, UU Zakat," *Neraca*, August 4, 1999.

174 Eri Sudewo, "Menyoroti Implementasi UU Zakat dan UU Pajak," *Republika*, October 27, 2000.

175 For example, FOZ organized a workshop entitled "Lokakarya Nasional Pokok-Pokok Materi RUU Zakat di Indonesia," held in Jakarta on July 15, 1999.

176 These four reasons are drawn from remarks made by the minister of religion at the DPR plenary session on the *zakat* bill, Jakarta, July 26, 1999 and recommendations made at the First Congress of FOZ, Jakarta, January 7–9, 1999.

177 Interview with Mukhtar Zarkasyi, Jakarta, September 11, 2003; interview with Isbir Fadly, Kasubdit Pemberdayaan Zakat (head of sub-directorate of *zakat* empowerment), Jakarta, September 3, 2003.

178 "Risalah Rapat Jum'at 3 September 1999," *Pembicaraan Tingkat III Pembahasan RUU tentang Pengelolaan Zakat* (Jakarta: Sekretariat Komisi VII Sekjen DPR RI, 1999), 20–25.

179 "Risalah Rapat Jum'at 3 September 1999," *Pembicaraan Tingkat III Pembahasan RUU tentang Pengelolaan Zakat* (Jakarta: Sekretariat Komisi VII Sekjen DPR RI, 1999), 26–27.

180 Interview with Didin Hafiduddin, Jakarta, August 30, 2003.

181 Interview with Dawam Rahardjo, Jakarta, August 28, 2003; for further details, see herein "*Zakat* and Tax: A Double Burden for Muslims."

182 Interview with Mukhtar Zarkasyi, Jakarta, September 11, 2003. The regulations referred to by Mukhtar were the 1925 Company Tax Ordinance and the 1944 Income Tax Ordinance.

183 See, e.g., Decree of the Minister for Finance No. KEP.650/MK/11/5/1976 and Circular Letter No. SE-11/PJ.62/1979 signed by General Director of Taxation Sutadi Sukarya. Both regulations were distributed at the bill deliberation by MORA in an attempt to stop parliamentary members from criticizing the proposed tax deductions in the *zakat* bill. Interview with Mukhtar Zarkasyi, Jakarta, September 11, 2003; cf. *Pembicaraan Tingkat III Pembahasan RUU tentang Pengelolaan Zakat* (Jakarta: Sekretariat Komisi VII Sekjen DPR RI, 1999).

184 The president's authority to settle disputes between ministries is based on Presidential Decree No. 188/1998.

185 Article 13, paragraph 2 of the *zakat* bill prepared by MORA stated, "*zakat yang telah dibayarkan kepada Badan Amil Zakat dikurangkan dari laba/pendapatan sisa kena pajak dari wajib pajak yang bersangkutan sesuai dengan peraturan yang berlaku.*"

186 Personal communication with Teten Kustiawan, Jakarta, September 2, 2003; cf.

"Pemandangan Umum Fraksi Reformasi," remarks made at "Discussion of Five Bills on the Amendment to the Laws of Taxation," House of Representatives, Jakarta, June 8, 2000; see also "Jawaban Pemerintah" remarks made at a similar program held on June 14, 2000. For the full text of these remarks, see *Pembahasan Lima Rancangan Undang-Undang tentang Perubahan uu di Bidang Perpajakan (Buku 1B)* (Jakarta: Sekjend DPR RI, PPPI, 2000).

187 "Pelaksanaan UU Zakat Belum Bisa Diterapkan Masyarakat," *Media Indonesia*, April 4, 2002. Didin Hafiduddin, a chairman of the Consultative Board of BAZNAS, the national board of *zakat* agencies, pointed out that the problem lies in implementing regulations under *zakat* law, which is a ministerial decree (KMA) issued by the minister of religion. In his view, there should be a Peraturan Pemerintah (PP) or government regulation to address the interdepartmental issue on *zakat* and tax. Interview with Didin Hafiduddin, Jakarta, August 30, 2003.

188 Cf. The form of Bukti Setoran Zakat issued by BAZNAS and the Decree of the General Directorate of Taxation on "Perlakuan Zakat atas Penghasilan dalam Penghitungan Penghasilan Kena Pajak Pajak Penghasilan."

189 M. Ikhsan, "Tithe and Tax Reduction," *The Jakarta Post*, December 5, 2001.

190 See, e.g., Eri Sudewo, "Mengkritisi UU Zakat," *Republika*, May 23, 2003; see also the decision made of the B Commission at the Third National Congress of FOZ, *Hasil Rumusan Musyawarah Nasional III Forum Zakat*, (Jakarta: FOZ, 2003), 4.

191 "Zakat Plan Questioned," *The Jakarta Post*, December 1, 2001.

192 "Tax Deduction of Zakat Must Apply to Non-Muslims," *The Jakarta Post*, November 29, 2001.

193 "Gov't Wants to Focus on Zakat First: Minister," *The Jakarta Post*, December 3, 2001.

194 See "Minutes of the meeting between FOZ and the Commission Six of DPR," Monday, January 28, 2002. A copy of this proceeding is available from the author.

195 This information comes from "Presentations of FOZ at the meeting between FOZ and the Commission Six of DPR," Jakarta, January 28, 2002. A copy of this presentation is available from the author.

196 See "Draft Usulan Amandemen UU no. 38 tahun 1999 tentang Pengelolaan Zakat." A copy of this draft is available from the author.

197 See Murasa Sarkaniputra, et al., "Respon Institusi Pengelola Zakat terhadap

Efektivitas Undang-Undang no. 38 tahun 1999" (Jakarta: Lembaga Penelitian UIN Syarif Hidayatullah, 2002/2003).

198 Djamal Doa is a former legislator of the Islamic Party (PPP).

199 Sunarsip is a freelance columnist.

200 See papers by Djamal Doa and Sunarsip, respectively, on the issue "Urgensi Amandemen Undang-Undang nomor 38/1999 tentang Pengelolaan Zakat dalam Konteks Pengentasan Kemiskinan," in *Hasil Rumusan Musyawarah Nasional III Forum Zakat* (Jakarta: FOZ, 2003), 75–83 and 93–95.

201 Tulus is director of *Zakat* and *Wakaf*, Ministry of Religious Affairs.

202 Wahiduddin Adam is director of the Harmonization of Regulations, the Ministry of Justice and Human Rights.

203 See papers by Tulus and Wahiduddin Adam respectively in *Hasil Rumusan Musyawarah Nasional III Forum Zakat* (Jakarta: FOZ, 2003), 71–74 and 84–92.

204 Wahiduddin Adam, "Amandemen Undang-Undang nomor 38 tahun 1999 tentang Pengelolaan Zakat: Dalam Perspektif Hukum," in *Hasil Rumusan Musyawarah Nasional III*, 90.

205 Ibid., 90–91.

206 See *Hasil Rumusan Musyawarah Nasional III*, 6–7.

207 See *Laporan Evaluasi Satu Tahun Kepengurusan Forum Zakat 1424 H*, Jakarta, April 2–3, 2004.

208 The overall votes for the Islamic parties in the 2004 election were less than 20 percent. See "Rekapitulasi Perolehan Suara Sah Untuk DPR RI," available at <http://www.kpu.go.id/suara/hasilsuara_dpr_sah.php> [accessed December 8, 2005].

209 According to a rough calculation made by BAZNAS, in 2003 the collection of *zakat* amounted to 350 billion *rupiahs*, most of it *zakat profesi*. Interview with Isbir Fadly, Jakarta, October 26, 2004.

LIST OF TERMS

ABRI	Armed Forces of the Republic of Indonesia
adat	localized traditional law and custom
Al-Irsyad	Muslim modernist movement
amil	a person or institution that manages the collection of *zakat*
BAZ	Badan Amil Zakat (official *zakat* agencies)
BAZIS	Badan Amil Zakat, Infak dan Sedekah (*zakat* collection board)
BAZNAS	Badan Amil Zakat Nasional (national board of *zakat* agencies)
bid'ah	religious heresies
Baitul Maal	Islamic Treasury
bupati	regent or head of district
DD	Dompet Dhuafa Republika (*zakat* agency created by Muslim community organizations); was a leading institution in the early establishment of FOZ
DPR-GR	Dewan Perwakilan Rakyat Gotong Royong (National Legislature); formed in the early New Order era
Golkar	Golongan Karya (Union of Functional Groups); an army-instituted and government-supported political party, which won over 60 percent of the vote in each of the elections held during the Suharto era. The term "functional groups" refers to groups within society such as peasants, workers, women, etc.
kepala desa	village head
LAZ	Lembaga Amil Zakat (non-state *zakat* agencies)
MIAI	Majlis Islam A'la Indonesia (pre-war federation of Islamic political parties and mass organizations)
MORA	Ministry of Religious Affairs

MPR	Majelis Permusyawaratan Rakyat (People's Consultative Assembly)
MPRS	Majelis Permusyawaratan Rakyat Sementara (Provincial People's Consultative Assembly)
Muhammadiyah	Muslim modernist movement
MUI	Majelis Ulama Indonesia (Indonesian Council of Islamic Scholars; also referred to as Indonesian Council of Ulama)
Muslim sejati	"true Muslims"
muzakki	*zakat* payers
nisab	minimum amount liable to *zakat* payment
NU	Nahdlatul Ulama (Ulama Awakening Organization); the largest Muslim organization founded in 1926 by K. H. Hasyim Asy'ari and K. H. Abdul Wahab Hasbullah
P3M	Perhimpunan Pesantren dan Masyarakat (Association for Pesantren [Islamic Boarding Schools] and Social Development)
PAD	*Pendapatan Asli Daerah* (Regional Basic Income); this refers to regional governments' revenue streams derived from local taxes, charges, fees, and revenue from local enterprises
PAN	Partai Amanat Nasional (National Mandate Party)
Persis	Muslim modernist movement
PKPU	Pos Keadilan Peduli Ummat (Justice Post of Muslim Care)
PMA	Perturan Menteri Agama (ministerial decree)
PP	Peraturan Pemerintah (government regulation)
PPP	Partai Persatuan Pembangunan (United Development Party)
RUU	Rancangan Undang-Undang (legislative bill)
SI	Sarekat Islam (Islamic Union); the first nationalist political party in Indonesia to gain wide popular support; founded in 1911
UPZ	Unit Pengumpul Zakat (*zakat* collector units)
wedana	district chief
zakat	a form of giving to those less fortunate in the Muslim community that is one of the Five Pillars of Islam; the required annual duty amounts to 2.5 percent of a person's wealth and assets

GOVERNMENT ADMINISTRATIONS
(1967–PRESENT)

Mar 1967–May 1998   Mohammed Suharto

May 1998–Oct 1999   B. J. Habibie

Oct 1999–Jul 2001   Abdurrahman Wahid (also known as Gus Dur)

Jul 2001–Oct 2004   Megawati Sukarno

Oct 2004–present   Susilo Bambang Yudhoyono

BIBLIOGRAPHY

Abdullah, Taufik. "Zakat Collection and Distribution in Indonesia." In *The Islamic Voluntary Sector in Southeast Asia,* edited by Mohammed Ariff. Singapore: ISEAS, 1991, 85–117.

Abu-Saud, Mahmoud. *Fiqh Al-Zakat Al-Mu'sir.* East Burnham, Bucks, UK: Oxford Publishing, 1989.

Adam, Wahiduddin. "Amandemen Undang-Undang nomor 38 tahun 1999 tentang Pengelolaan Zakat: Dalam Perspektif Hukum." In *Hasil Rumusan Musyawarah Nasional III Forum Zakat: Menggagas Amandemen uu no. 38 tahun 1999 tentang Pengelolaan Zakat, Menuju Optimalisasi Dana Zakat, Balikpapan, 25–28 April 2003.* Jakarta: FOZ, 2003.

Al-Attas, S. M. N. *Preliminary Statement on a General Theory of Islamization of the Malay-Indonesian Archipelago.* Kuala Lumpur: Dewan Bahasa dan Pustaka, 1969.

Aminuddin. *Kekuatan Islam dan Pergulatan Kekuasaan di Indonesia: Sebelum dan Sesudah Runtuhnya Rezim Soeharto.* Yogyakarta: Pustaka Pelajar, 1999.

Ansari, Abdul Rehman. *Zakat: the Religious Tax of Islam.* Durban, South Africa: Premier Press, 1973.

Anshari, Endang Saefuddin. *Piagam Jakarta 22 Juni 1945.* Jakarta: Rajawali Press, 1986.

Anwar, Marzani. "BAZIS DKI Jakarta: Sosok Keamilan Modern." *Pesantren* 3, no. 2 (1986).

Awwas, Irfan S., ed. *Risalah Kongres Mujahidin I dan Penegakan Syari'ah Islam.* Yogyakarta: Wihdah Press, 2001.

Azra, Azyumardi. *Renaisans Islam Asia Tenggara: Sejarah Wacana dan Kekuasaan.* Bandung: Remaja Rosdakarya, 1999.

Azra, Azyumardi, and Saiful Umam, eds. *Menteri-Menteri Agama RI: Biografi Sosial Politik.* Jakarta: INIS-PPIM-Balitbang Depag RI, 1998.

Bajunid, O. Farouk. "Islam and State in Southeast Asia." In *State and Islam,* edited by C. van Dijk and A. H. de Groot. Leiden: Research School CNWS, 1995.

Bakti, Andi Faisal. *Islam and Nation Formation in Indonesia: From Communitarian to Organizational Communications.* Jakarta: Logos, 2000.

Bashear, Suliman. "On the Origins and Development of the Meaning of Zakat in Early Islam." *Arabica* 40 (1993): 84–113.

Benda, Harry J. "Christiaan Snouck Hurgronje and the Foundations of Dutch

Islamic Policy in Indonesia." *The Journal of Modern History* 30 (December 1958): 338–347.

———. *The Crescent and the Rising Sun: Indonesia Under the Japanese Occupation, 1942–1945.* The Hague/Bandung: W. van Hoeve, 1958.

Benthall, Jonathan. "Financial Worship: The Qur'anic Injunction to Almsgiving." *Journal of the Royal Anthropological Institute* 5 (March 1999): 27–42.

Boland, B. J. *The Struggle of Islam in Modern Indonesia.* The Hague: Martinus Nijhoff, 1982.

Braten, Eldar. "To Colour, Not Oppose: Spreading Islam in Rural Java." In *Muslim Diversity: Local Islam in Global Contexts*, edited by Leif Manger. Surrey: Curzon, 1999.

Clark, Grace. "Pakistan's Zakat and 'Ushr as a Welfare System." In *Islamic Reassertion in Pakistan: The Application of Islamic Laws in a Modern State*, edited by Anita M. Weiss. Syracuse: Syracuse University Press, 1986, 79–95.

Cummings, W. "Scripting Islamization: Arabic Texts in Early Modern Makassar." *Ethnohistory* 48, no. 4 (2001): 559–586.

Damanik, Ali Said. *Fenomena Partai Keadilan: Transformasi 20 Tahun Gerakan Tarbiyah di Indonesia.* Jakarta: Teraju, 2002.

Daradjat, Zakiah. *Zakat: Pembersih Harta Dan Jiwa.* Jakarta: YPI Ruhana, 1991.

de Zayas, Farishta G. *The Law and Philosophy of Zakat; the Islamic Social Welfare System.* Damascus: al-Jadidah Printing Press, 1960.

Doa, Djamal. *Menggagas Pengelolaan Zakat oleh Negara.* Jakarta: Nuansa Madani, 2001.

Dobbin, C. *Islamic Revivalism in a Changing Peasant Economy: Central Sumatra 1784–1847.* London: Curzon, 1983.

Drewes, G. W. J. *An Early Javanese Code of Muslim Ethics.* The Hague: Martinus Nijhoff, 1978.

———. "New Light on the Coming of Islam to Indonesia?" *Bijdragen tot de Taal-, Land-en Volkenkunde* 124 (1968): 433–459.

Effendy, Bahtiar. *Islam dan Negara: Transformasi Pemikiran dan Praktik Politik Islam di Indonesia.* Jakarta: Paramadina, 1998.

Fadlullah. *Mengenal Hukum ZIS dan Pengamalannya di DKI Jakarta.* Jakarta: BAZIS DKI, 1993.

Federspiel, H. M. *Persatuan Islam: Islamic Reform in Twentieth Century Indonesia.* Ithaca, New York: Cornell University, Modern Indonesia Project, 1970.

Feillard, Andree. *NU vis-à-vis Negara: Pencarian Isi, Bentuk dan Makna.* Translated from *Islam et Armee Dans L'Indonesie Contemporaine Les Pionners de la tradition.* Yogjakarta: LKIS, 1995.

Geertz, Clifford. *Islam Observed: Religious Development in Morocco and Indonesia.* Chicago: University of Chicago Press, 1968.

———. *The Religion of Java.* New York: The Free Press, 1960.

Gobee, E., and C. Adriannse, eds. *Ambtelijk Adviezen van C. Snouck Hurgronje 1889–1936.* 's-Gravenhage: Martinus Nijhoff, 1957.

Hafiduddin, Didin. *Zakat dalam Perekonomian Modern.* Jakarta: Gema Insani Press, 2002.

Hamidiyah, Emmy. "Refleksi Tiga Tahun Baznas." In *Hasil Rumusan Lokakarya Nasional Regulasi dan Pengawasan Pengelolaan Zakat di Indonesia: Menghitung Peran Strategis Baznas.* Jakarta: FOZ, 2003.

Hefner, Robert W. "Islamizing Capitalism: On the Founding of Indonesia's First Islamic Bank." In *Towards a New Paradigm: Recent Developments in Indonesian Islamic Thought,* edited by Mark Woodward and J. Rush. Tempe: Arizona State University Program of Southeast Asian Studies, 1995, 291–322.

———. "Islamizing Java?: Religion and Politics in Rural East Java." *The Journal of Asian Studies* 46, no. 3 (1987): 533–554.

Hisyam, Muhammad. *Caught Between Three Fires: The Javanese Pangulu Under the Dutch Colonial Administration 1882–1942.* Jakarta: INIS, 2001.

Hooker, M. B. "The Translation of Islam into South-East Asia." In *Islam in South-East Asia,* edited by M. B. Hooker. Leiden: E. J. Brill, 1983.

Hurgronje, Christiaan Snouck. *Nasihat-Nasihat C. Snouck Hurgronje Semasa Kepegawaiannya kepada Pemerintah Hindia Belanda 1880–1936.* Translated by Sukarsi from *Ambtelijk Adviezen van C. Snouck Hurgronje 1889–1936,* edited by E. Gobee and C. Adriannse. Jakarta: INIS, 1992.

Idris, Sofwan. *Gerakan Zakat dalam Pemberdayaan Ekonomi Umat:Pendekatan Transformatif.* Jakarta: Cita Putra Bangsa, 1997.

Ikhsan, M. "Tithe and Tax Reduction." *The Jakarta Post,* December 5, 2001.

Jehle, Geoffrey A. "Zakat and Inequality: Some Evidence from Pakistan." *The Review of Income and Wealth* 40 (June 1994): 205–216.

Karim, M. Rusli. *Negara dan Peminggiran Islam Politik.* Yogyakarta: Tiara Wacana, 1999.

Kepel, Gilles. *Jihad: The Trail of Political Islam.* Translated by Anthony F. Roberts. Cambridge, Massachusetts: The Belknap Press of Harvard University Press, 2002.

Kuran, Timur. "Islamic Redistribution through Zakat: Historical Record and Modern Realities." In *Poverty and Charity in Middle Eastern Contexts,* edited by Michael Bonner, Mine Ener, and Amy Singer. Albany: State University of New York Press, 2002, 275–293.

———. "The Economic Impact of Islamic Fundamentalism." In *Fundamentalisms and the State: Remaking Polities, Economies and Militance,* edited by M. Marty and S. Appleby. Chicago: University of Chicago Press, 1993, 302–341.

Kuraysha, A. T. Abu. *Al-Zakat wa al-Tanmiya.* Cairo, 1999. Cited in A. Zysow, "Zakat," *The Encylopaedia of Islam,* New Edition, vol. 11, 2002.

Ma'arif, Syafi'i. *Islam dan Masalah Kenegaraan: Studi Tentang Percaturan dalam Konstituante.* Jakarta: LP3ES, 1985.

Malik, Jamal. *Colonialization of Islam: Dissolution of Traditional Institutions in Pakistan.* New Delhi: Manohar, 1996.

Marijan, Kacung. "Islamization of Java: From Hindu-Buddhist Kingdoms to New Order Indonesia." *Jurnal Studi Indonesia* 8, no. 2 (1998).

Mas'udi, Masdar F. *Agama Keadilan: Risalah Zakat (Pajak) dalam Islam.* Jakarta: P3M, 1991.

Masykuri, Abdillah. *Responses of Indonesian Muslim Intellectuals to the Concept of Democracy.* Hamburg: Abera Network Austronesia, 1997.

Mayer, Ann Elizabeth. "The Fundamentalist Impact on Law, Politics and Constitutions in Iran, Pakistan and the Sudan." In *Fundamentalism and The State: Remaking Polities, Economies and Militance,* edited by Martin E. Marty and R. Scott Appleby. Chicago and London: University of Chicago Press, 1993, 110–151.

———. "Islamization and Taxation in Pakistan." In *Islamic Reassertion in Pakistan: The Application of Islamic Laws in a Modern State,* edited by Anita M. Weiss. Syracuse: Syracuse University Press, 1986, 59–77.

———. "Law and Religion in the Muslim Middle East." *The American Journal of Comparative Law* 35 (1987): 127–184.

Milner, A. C. "Islam and the Muslim State." In *Islam in South-East Asia,* edited by M. B. Hooker. Leiden: E. J. Brill, 1983, 23–49.

Moejanto, G. *The Concept of Power in Javanese Culture.* Yogyakarta: Gadjah Mada University Press, 1990.

Mufty, Aries. "Kemandirian Umat Islam Melalui Konsolidasi ZIS dalam Rangka Mengoptimalkan Pemberdayaan ZIS." In *Hasil Rumusan Lokakarya Nasional Regulasi dan Pengawasan Pengelolaan Zakat di Indonesia: Menghitung Peran Strategis Baznas.* Jakarta: FOZ, 2003.

Muhammad, Sahri. *Pengembangan Zakat dan Infak dalam Upaya Meningkatkan Kesejahteraan Masyarakat.* Malang: Yayasan Pusat Studi Avicena, 1982.

Muzaffar, Chandra. "Islamisation of State and Society: Some Further Critical Remarks." In *Shari'a Law and the Modern Nation-State,* edited by Norani Othman. Kuala Lumpur: Sisters in Islam, 1994, 113–122.

Nasution, Adnan Buyung. *The Aspiration for Constitutional Government in Indo-*

nesia: A Socio-Legal Study of the Indonesian Konstituante 1956–1959. Jakarta: Pustaka Sinar Harapan, 1992.

Noer, Deliar. *Gerakan Modern Islam di Indonesia 1900–1942*. Jakarta: LP3ES, 1980.

Noorduyn, J. "Makasar and the Islamization of Bima." *Bijdragen tot de Taal-, Land-en Volkenkunde* 143 (1987): 312–342.

Novossyolov, Dimitri B. "The Islamization of Welfare in Pakistan." In *Russia's Muslim Frontiers: New Directions in Cross-Cultural Analysis*, edited by Dale F. Eickelman. Bloomington and Indianapolis: Indiana University Press, 1993, 160–174.

Peacock J. L. *Purifying the Faith: The Muhammadiyah Movement in Indonesian Islam*. California: Cummings Publishing Company, 1978.

Pelras, Christian. "Religion, Tradition and the Dynamics of Islamization in South Sulawesi." *Archipel* 29 (1985): 107–135.

Permono, Sjechul Hadi. *Pemerintah Republik Indonesia Sebagai Pengelola Zakat*. Jakarta: Pustaka Firdaus, 1993.

―――. "Pola Pemikiran Zakat Badan Amil Zakat, Infaq Shadaqah (BAZIS) DKI Jakarta." Master's thesis, IAIN Syarif Hidayatullah, Jakarta, 1984.

Rahardjo, Dawam. "Manajemen Zakat." In *Pedoman Pembinaan BAZIS: Hasil Pertemuan Nasional I BAZIS Se-Indonesia tanggal 3–4 Maret 1992*. Jakarta: Bimas Islam dan Urusan Haji, 1992.

―――. *Perspektif Deklarasi Makkah: Menuju Ekonomi Islam*. Bandung: Mizan, 1987.

Ricklefs, Merle C. *History of Modern Indonesia since c. 1200*. Stanford: Stanford University Press, 2001.

―――. "Six Centuries of Islamization in Java." In *Conversion to Islam*, edited by N. Levtzion. New York: Holmes and Meir, 1979, 100–128.

Rossler, Martin. "Islamization and the Reshaping of Identities in Rural South Sulawesi." In *Islam in an Era of Nation-States: Politics and Religious Renewal in Muslim Southeast Asia*, edited by Robert W. Hefner and Patricia Horvatich. Honolulu: Hawai'i University Press, 1997, 275–308.

Rouffaer, G. P. "Vorstenlanden." In *Adatrechtbundels*, vol. 34, *Java en Madoera*. 's-Gravenhage: Martinus Nijhoof, 1931.

Salim, Arskal. "Shari'a in Indonesia's Current Transition: An Update." In *Shari'a and Politics of Modern Indonesia*, edited by Arskal Salim and Azyumardi Azra. Singapore: ISEAS, 2003, 213–232.

―――. "*Zakat* Administration in Politics of Indonesian New Order." In *Shari'a and Politics in Modern Indonesia*, edited by Arskal Salim and Azyumardi Azra. Singapore: ISEAS, 2003, 181–192.

Salleh, Muhammad Syukri. "Islamisation of State and Society: A Critical Comment." In *Shari'a Law and the Modern Nation-State*, edited by Norani Othman. Kuala Lumpur: Sisters in Islam, 1994, 106–111.

Sarkaniputra, Murasa, et al. "Respon Institusi Pengelola Zakat terhadap Efektivitas Undang-Undang no. 38 tahun 1999." Jakarta: Lembaga Penelitian UIN Syarif Hidayatullah, 2002/2003.

Scott, James C. "Resistance Without Protest and Without Organization: Peasant Opposition to the Islamic Zakat and the Christian Tithe." *Comparative Studies in Society and History* 29, no. 3 (July 1987): 417–452.

Steenbrink, Karel. *Beberapa Aspek Tentang Islam di Indonesia Abad ke-19*. Jakarta: Bulan Bintang, 1984.

———. *Dutch Colonialism and Indonesian Islam: Contacts and Conflicts, 1596–1950*. Amsterdam-Atlanta, GA : Rodopi B. V., 1993.

Sudewo, Eri. "Ahlan Wa Sahlan, UU Zakat." *Neraca*, August 4, 1999.

———. "Keterkaitan UU no. 38/1999 dengan UU no. 17/2000: Sebuah Pergeseran Paradigma." In *Problematika Zakat Kontemporer: Artikulasi Proses Sosial Politik Bangsa*, edited by Muhtar Sadili and Amru. Jakarta: FOZ, 2003.

———. "Lembaga Regulator dan Pengawas Pengelolaan Zakat." In *Hasil Rumusan Lokakarya Nasional Regulasi dan Pengawasan Pengelolaan Zakat di Indonesia: Menghitung Peran Strategis Baznas*. Jakarta: FOZ, 2003.

———. "Mengkritisi UU Zakat." *Republika*, May 23, 2003.

———. "Menyoroti Implementasi UU Zakat dan UU Pajak." *Republika*, October 27, 2000.

Suminto, Aqib. *Politik Islam Hindia Belanda*. Jakarta: LP3ES, 1985.

Surur, Naharus. "Baznas Masa Depan." In *Hasil Rumusan Lokakarya Nasional Regulasi dan Pengawasan Pengelolaan Zakat di Indonesia: Menghitung Peran Strategis Baznas*. Jakarta: FOZ, 2003.

Sutarmadi, Ahmad. "Unifikasi dan Nasionalisasi Manajemen Pengelolaan Zakat Infak Shadaqah." Paper presented at the national seminar on "Rekonseptualisasi Strategi Pendayagunaan Zakat untuk Pembangunan Ekonomi yang Berkeadilan dan Berkerakyatan untuk Menyongsong Abad 21," Faculty of Syariah IAIN Syarif Hidayatullah Jakarta, March 25–26, 1997.

Syarief, Hidayat. "Pendayagunaan Institusi Zakat sebagai Alternatif Pemberdayaan Ekonomi Rakyat." Paper presented at the national seminar on "Rekonseptualisasi Strategi Pendayagunaan Zakat untuk Pembangunan Ekonomi yang Berkeadilan dan Berkerakyatan untuk Menyongsong Abad 21", Faculty of Syariah IAIN Syarif Hidayatullah Jakarta, March 25–26, 1997.

Syihab, Habib M. Rizieq. *Dialog Piagam Jakarta: Kumpulan Jawaban*. Jakarta: Pustaka Ibnu Sidah, 2000.

Thaba, Abdul Azis. *Islam dan Negara dalam Politik Orde Baru.* Jakarta: Gema Insani Press, 1996.

Thalib, Sayuti. *Receptio in Contrario.* Jakarta: Bina Aksara, 1982.

Tonang, Andi Lolo. "Beberapa Pemikiran tentang Mekanisme Badan Amil Zakat." In *Zakat dan Pajak,* edited by B. Wiwoho. Jakarta: PT Bina Rena Pariwara, 1992.

van Bruinessen, Martin. "Genealogies of Islamic Radicalism in Post-Suharto Indonesia." *South East Asia Research* 10, no. 2 (2002): 117–154.

———. "Shari'a Court, Tarekat and Pesantren: Religious Administration in the Banten Sultanate." *Archipel* 50 (1995): 166–199.

van Dijk, C. *Rebellion under the Banner of Islam: The Darul Islam in Indonesia.* The Hague: Martinus Nijhoff, 1981.

Woodward, Mark R. *Islam in Java: Normative Piety and Mysticism in Sultanate of Yogyakarta.* Tucson: University of Arizona Press, 1989.

Ybarra, Josep-Antoni. "The Zaqat in Muslim Society: An Analysis of Islamic Economic Policy." *Social Science Information* 35 (1996): 643–656.

Zada, Khamami. *Islam Radikal: Pergulatan Ormas-Ormas Islam Garis Keras di Indonesia.* Jakarta: Teraju, 2002.

Zulkarnain, Iskandar. "BAZNAS Sebuah Catatan: Awal yang tertatih-tatih." INFOZ, edition no. 3, Muharram, March 14–25, 2004.

———. "Pentingnya Jaringan Kerja Antar Lembaga Pengelola Zakat untuk Mengatasi Problematika Ummat." Paper presented at Semiloka Dai dan Muballigh Se-Jabotebek, March 1, 2003.

Newspapers

The Jakarta Post. "Gov't Wants to Focus on Zakat First: Minister," December 3, 2001.

———. "Tax Deduction of Zakat Must Apply to Non-Muslims," November 29, 2001.

———. "Zakat Plan Questioned," December 1, 2001.

Media Indonesia. "Pelaksanaan UU Zakat Belum Bisa Diterapkan Masyarakat," April 4, 2002.

Republika. "Baznas Kerja Sama dengan PNM," August 10, 2002.

———. "BUMN Enggan Jadi Unit Pengumpul Zakat," June 6, 2003.

———. "Menag Tak Izinkan Pendirian LAZ Baru," June 3, 2003.

Non-State and Government Publications

Direktori Lembaga Amil Zakat. Jakarta: Direktorat Pengembangan Zakat dan Wakaf, 2003.

Direktori Organisasi Pengelola Zakat di Indonesia. Jakarta: FOZ, 2001.

Hasil Rumusan Musyawarah Kerja Nasional I Lembaga Pengelola ZIS. Jakarta: FOZ, 1999.

Hasil Rumusan Musyawarah Nasional III Forum Zakat: Menggagas Amandemen UU no. 38 tahun 1999 tentang Pengelolaan Zakat, Menuju Optimalisasi Dana Zakat, Balikpapan, 25–28 April 2003. Jakarta: FOZ, 2003.

Laporan Evaluasi Satu Tahun Kepengurusan Forum Zakat 1424 H. Jakarta: FOZ, 2004.

Pedoman Pembinaan BAZIS: Hasil Pertemuan Nasional I BAZIS se-Indonesia tanggal 3–4 Maret 1992. Jakarta: Dirjen Bimas Islam Urusan Haji Departemen Agama, 1992.

Pedoman Zakat. Jakarta: Proyek Pembinaan Zakat dan Wakaf, 1992/1993.

Pembahasan Lima Rancangan Undang-Undang tentang Perubahan UU di Bidang Perpajakan (Buku 1B). Jakarta: Sekjend DPR RI, PPPI, 2000.

Pembicaraan Tingkat III Pembahasan RUU tentang Pengelolaan Zakat. Jakarta: Sekretariat Komisi VII Sekjen DPR RI, 1999.

Pola Kecenderungan Masyarakat Berzakat. Jakarta: PIRAC, 2002.

Profil Direktorat Pengembangan Zakat dan Wakaf. Jakarta: Dep. Agama, 2003.

"Risalah Rapat Jum'at 3 September 1999." In *Pembicaraan Tingkat III Pembahasan RUU tentang Pengelolaan Zakat.* Jakarta: Sekretariat Komisi VII Sekjen DPR RI, 1999.

Interviews

Interview with Amru (former staff member of FOZ), Jakarta, October 20, 2004.

Interview with Dawam Rahardjo (Muhammadiyah intellectual), Jakarta, August 28, 2003.

Interview with Didin Hafiduddin (chairman of BAZNAS), Jakarta, August 30, 2003.

Interview with Isbir Fadly, Kasubdit Pemberdayaan Zakat (head of sub-directorate of zakat empowerment), Jakarta, September 3, 2003.

Interview with Iskandar Zulkarnain (former chairman of FOZ), Jakarta, September 4, 2003.

Interview with Masdar F. Mas'udi (vice chairman of Nahdlatul Ulama), Jakarta, August 19, 1999 and August 25, 2003.

Interview with Miftahul Munir (former head of sub-directorate of zakat and wakaf, MORA), Jakarta, August 27, 2003.

Interview with Mukhtar Zarkasyi (former senior official of MORA), Jakarta, September 11, 2003.

ISLAM IN SOUTHEAST ASIA: VIEWS FROM WITHIN
Research Fellowship Program for Young Muslim Scholars

The fellowship program aims to enhance understanding of Islam in Southeast Asia from an "insider's perspective" while building the research capacity of young Muslim scholars and offering them publishing opportunities. Small grants are awarded annually for innovative research on issues concerning socio-political and cultural changes taking place in the diverse Muslim communities of Southeast Asia, especially as they relate to modernization and globalization. Key themes include: popular manifestations of Islam; shaping of Muslim identities in Southeast Asia by regional and globalizing forces; changing gender dynamics in Muslim communities; and the way Islamic values inform economic activities and social responsibilities.

Initiated in 2002, the program is managed by the secretariat of the Asian Muslim Action Network (AMAN) in Bangkok, Thailand, with the advice of leading experts from the region and the financial support of the Rockefeller Foundation.

Information on the program and how to apply can be found at
http://fellowship.arf-asia.org/

AMAN/ARF
House 1562/113, Soi 1/1
Mooban Pibul, Pracharaj Road
Bangkok 10800, Thailand

Tel: 66-2-9130196
Fax: 66-2-9130197

E-mail: aman@arf-asia.org
http://www.arf-asia.org/aman